DAVID LEE is Senior Assistant Editor of *The Scotsman* and has worked for the paper in various executive roles for eight years. He edits the paper's specialist professional pages, writes an irreverent column every Monday, compiles the daily diary – and, of course, edits *Recommends* on Wednesdays.

He has been involved in a wide range of other high-profile editorial projects, including the Seven Wonders of Scotland, which attracted one of the paper's biggest-ever reader responses as 50,000 votes were cast to find what people loved best about their country. David also organised *The Scotsman's* hugely ambitious project to mark the 300th anniversary of the Treaty of Union. Under the 'Scotland 300' banner, the paper hosted eight nationhood debates across the country and sent reporters out to more than 20 towns to ask people what Scotland meant to them in 2007.

Away from work, David is a harassed father of four children and coaches a youth football team.

Scotland Recommends

The Word-of-Mouth Guide to Scotland

Edited by
DAVID LEE

Luath Press Limited

EDINBURGH

www.luath.co.uk

First published 2008

ISBN (10): 1-906307-47-4
ISBN (13): 978-1-906307-47-9

The paper used in this book is recyclable. It is manufactured from
woodpulp from sustainable forests.

Printed and bound by Scotprint, Haddington

Typeset in Frutiger by 3btype.com

Design by Tom Bee

Map by Jim Lewis

CONTENTS

Preface		7
Best First Birthday Poem		9
Acknowledgements		11
1	Caves	13
2	Delicatessens	13
3	Bookshops	14
4	Fish and chips	15
5	Self-catering cottages	15
6	Cheap places to eat	16
7	Places to skim stones	18
8	Family walks	19
9	Ice cream	20
10	Sandwich bars	20
11	Munros for novices	21
12	Playparks	23
13	Italian restaurants	24
14	Traditional music venues	25
15	Robert Burns sites	25
16	Real cider pubs	26
17	Winter youth hostels	27
18	Free things to do with children	28
19	Places to see owls	28
20	Brochs	30
21	Dive sites	31
22	French restaurants	32
23	Birdwatching sites	33
24	Butchers	34
25	Wild places	34
26	Farm shops/farmers' markets	36
27	Independent wine shops	38
28	Glasshouses	39
29	Quiet beaches	40
30	Style bars	42
31	Gardens	43
32	Crêpes	44
33	High-level drives	45
34	Old-fashioned pubs	46
35	Spots for stargazing	47
36	Breakfasts	48
37	Chocolatiers	48
38	Train journeys	49
39	Romantic restaurants	50
40	Hidden shopping gems	52
41	Island towns	52
42	Places to see salmon leaping	53
43	Boating ponds	55
44	City viewpoints	56
45	Cheese shops	57
46	Victorian spa towns	57
47	Fishing for beginners	58
48	Sweet shops	59
49	Seafood restaurants	59
50	Places for teenagers to eat	60
51	Great roads for bikers	61
52	Pre-theatre meals	62
53	Toyshops	63
54	Rugby grounds	63
55	Toilets	64
56	Surfing beaches	65
57	Walkers' bars	66
58	Wishing wells and trees	67
59	Film locations	68
60	Japanese food	70
61	Birthplaces to visit	71
62	Sunday lunches	72
63	Small cinemas	73
64	Places to build sandcastles	73
65	Climbing for beginners	75
66	Waterside walks	76
67	Bed and breakfasts	78
68	Roadside food	78
69	Shoe shops	79
70	Pine forests	80
71	Campsites	81
72	Places to find conkers	81
73	Extreme points of Scotland	82
74	Great wedding locations	83
75	Afternoon teas	85
76	Florists	85
77	Places to see autumn leaves	86

78	Indian food	87
79	Famous trees	88
80	Vegetarian restaurants	89
81	Contemporary buildings	89
82	Sports shops	91
83	Fairtrade clothes	92
84	Days out on Royal Deeside	92
85	Watercolour artists	93
86	Hotel bars	94
87	Places to propose	95
88	Country house hotels	96
89	Coffee shops	96
90	Sailing and fine dining	97
91	Glens	98
92	Sealife centres	99
93	Scots words	99
94	Places to see the red deer rut	100
95	Jazz venues	103
96	Pizzas	104
97	Museums	105
98	Ferry journeys	105
99	Cathedrals	106
100	Fishing villages	108
101	Outdoor activity operators	109
102	All-day walks	110
103	Seabird-watching	110
104	Bike rides	113
105	Chinese food	113
106	War memorials	114
107	Places to see red squirrels	115
108	Alternative tourist attractions	116
109	Dog-friendly hotels	118
110	Places to fly kites	119
111	Shops to buy Christmas decorations	120
112	Country parks	120
113	Edin-burgers	122
114	Coastal painters	123
115	Cheap golf hotels	124
116	Places for steam enthusiasts	124
117	Cafés	125
118	Coastal walks	126
119	Intriguing place names	127
120	Places to buy Christmas cards	128

121	Waterfalls	129
122	Places to feed ducks	129
123	Dog walking	130
124	À la carte eating	131
125	Land-based dolphin watching	132
126	Garden centres	132
127	Lochs	133
128	Sculptures	135
129	Runs	136
130	Thai food	136
131	Places to see rare butterflies	137
132	Overnight stays for bikers	138
133	Woodland walks	139
134	Fishmongers	139
135	Green holidays	140
136	Geological wonders	141
137	Nine-hole golf courses	143

Index by category	146
Map of areas	148
Index by area	149

PREFACE

RECOMMENDS was launched as a weekly supplement in *The Scotsman* on 18 April 2007. Its aim was simple – to celebrate the very best of Scotland by giving readers a platform to tell others about their favourite places and experiences.

There were those who said it wouldn't last, that the store of recommendations wasn't deep enough to sustain more than a few months at most. I have to admit that I wasn't sure we'd be here more than a year later, with new and old recommenders constantly coming up with original categories to keep *Recommends* fresh.

This book is a collection of some of the best – and most useful – categories that have appeared in the supplement over the last year. While the weekly *Recommends* has at times verged on the bizarre and surreal, we have tried to make this book as practical as possible, while still retaining the quirkiness and humour of contributors. Some recommendations are in the first person, to reflect the personal experience of the writer.

You can use this book in several ways – treat it as a 'pick and mix' of the best of Scotland and dip in and out as you wish. Alternatively, use the alphabetical index at the back to find a category that interests you – or go to the geographical index (and map) at the back to find ideas on what to look for in a particular area.

Please remember that places come and go – and while mountains and waterfalls aren't likely to disappear any time soon, there is always a chance a coffee shop or Chinese restaurant might close, move or change its name. We have taken all precautions to ensure the information in this book is up to date, but cannot be held responsible for any disappointment arising from the recommendations.

This is not meant to be an exhaustive guide, but it is hopefully a useful, and slightly charming, book about the best Scotland has to offer. I would particularly like to thank Robert Ritchie, Steve McCabe and Lorraine Simpson for their regular and excellent recommendations and Peter Ranscombe, Liz Leydon and Matt Brereton of *The Scotsman* for their constant support and stream of ideas. The contributors to this book are a mixture of *Scotsman* staff and readers who share a common goal – to pass on their personal experiences about what is good about Scotland. Most categories are in top fives, which we have found to be ideal for chunky, bite-sized recommendations. Some are top tens instead, others are slightly different numbers – in these cases, they are often amalgamations of different contributors' choices.

No view is more or less valid than another – and if you have eaten in a superb bistro, stayed in a fantastic B&B or discovered a gem of a beach, we would love to hear from you. Please send us your recommendations by emailing **readersrecommend@scotsman.com** or writing to me at *The Scotsman*, 108 Holyrood Road, Edinburgh, EH8 8AS – or by logging on to **www.scotsman.com/recommends**

Happy reading.

David Lee
Assistant Editor
The Scotsman

BEST FIRST BIRTHDAY POEM

Pressed on these hallowed Holyrood
  Road sheets,
lying around the Woden's Day centre-
  fold,
there's no griping swiping flyting
  sniping slighting on this our supple,
  meant-well supplement:
categorically the best, a feel-good
  factory, the hale mixter-maxter,
  jing-bang, categlorious clanjamfrey;
  this hoachin, stoatin, kaleidoscopic,
  cornucopic, smorgasborgic, pot-
  pourric copy beano, this hotbed of
  unbridled best-reality

– and these are our sexalogue, our six
  commendments: thou shall be
  invigorated to action,
inspirited to visitation,
nourished with information,
tempted to titteration,
seduced to reflection,
induced to recollection –

let bells ring dong, and ding this
  spiel:
blessed be our band of sistern, and of
  brethren,
aiders and abesters in this mad glad
  venture,
citizen army of commenders,
  informed selectorate;
and blessed, but not least, the
  orchestrator,
our rightening conductor, surelee the
  best.

So let this ode sing out,
con-grat-u-lay-shons and cel-i-bray-
  shons,
on this our initial natalitial bash,
our one and only single-candle-cake
  day,
no wreck, no need of mends,
this muckle-splendoured, strongly
  weekly showing, best-loved
  melange that is *The Scotsman
  Recommends*!

ROBERT J RITCHIE

ACKNOWLEDGEMENTS

THANK YOU to all contributors to *Recommends* – if anyone who has contributed to this book been missed out, many apologies, but here are those who have definitely helped out with the recommending:

Barbara Agnew, Amy Bell, Jane Bradley, Craig Brown, Matt Brereton, Susan Burrell, Hazel Cameron, Stevie Christie, Emma Cowing, Roger Cox, Nic Crawshaw, Jason Cumming, Alasdair Currie, Don Currie, Abigail Daly, Alastair Dalton, Lindsay Dalton Hopwood, Tim Donald, Sandra Donnan, Charles Duncan, Andrew Eaton, John Ellingham, Louise Fairbairn, Stuart Farquhar, David Ferguson, David Findlay, Sarah Fletcher, Jim Gilchrist, Mike Gilson, Stuart Glen, Jenny Glumoff, Stuart Goodall, Charlotte Gosling, Paul Greaves, Michael Howie, Jackie Hunter, Kevin Hutchens, Doug Jackson, Ian Johnston, Phil Johnston, Jessica Kiddle, Ginny Lawson, Colin Leslie, Liz Leydon, Hamish Macdonell, Fiona Macleod, Paul MacMichael, Chris Marks, Derek McAdam, Steve McCabe, Jim McDonald, David McIntosh, Lindsay McIntosh, Kirsty McLuckie, Roger McStravick, Alan Nairn, Richard Paterson, Peter Ranscombe, James Reynolds, Robert Ritchie, David Robinson, David Rosenthal, Shan Ross, Ross Russell, Lorraine Simpson, Annie Shirra, Will Slater, Claire Smith, Rowan Smith, Gaby Soutar, Alan Steadman, Gabe Stewart, Ian Stewart, Annie and Brian Sutherland, Mary Taylor, Alison Turnbull, Andrea Vance, Donald Walker, Elise Walker, Sharon Ward, Sandra Wilkinson, Adam Wilson and Alice Wyllie.

1 CAVES

1 BONE CAVES HIGHLANDS
Inchnadamph
*www.walking.visitscotland.com/walks/
northhighlands/214500*
These four north-facing bone caves of
the Inchnadamph National Nature
Reserve look out from the base of the
limestone Creag nan Uamh over the
Allt nan Uamh glen in Wester Ross.
A wonderful walk on a good path and a
last scramble takes you back 7,000 years
to the bone caves, one of the earliest
sites of habitation in Scotland. Remains
of animals such as bear, lynx, wolf and
Arctic fox have been found there.
On the way, you pass by the entrance
to the largest underground cave system
in Scotland, but they're for experienced
cavers.

2 WEMYSS CAVES PAD&F
East Wemyss, Fife
www.wemysscaves.co.uk
Home of the famous Pictish carved
artwork, these include Court Cave,
Dovecote Cave, Jonathan's Cave and
Sliding Cave. Access is restricted,
however, to protect the carvings, so
check the website for details.

3 KING'S CAVE SOUTH SCOT
Arran *www.visitarran.net*
(click on Blackwaterfoot)
North of Blackwaterfoot on the west
coast of Arran is the cave made famous
by Robert the Bruce. According to
legend, it is the refuge in which he had
his famed encounter with a spider. It is
set above eight miles of raised beach,
and was formed about 6,000 years ago.
A beautiful gate protects it, but it is
usually open. There is also the challenge
of finding all the 15 caves in the vicinity.

4 GLENDRIAN CAVE HIGHLANDS
Ardnamurchan *(north-east of Sanna
Bay) www.cavedatabase.co.uk*
Found in a fissure in the cliffs, this is a
real *Indiana Jones* cave. It's a bit of a
squeeze at the start, but opens out and
goes a good way into cliff – look out
for the 'graffiti' dating back centuries,
and don't forget a torch.

5 OSSIAN'S CAVE SOUTH SCOT
Arran *www.cavedatabase.co.uk*
(use Advanced Search)
Three kilometres along the coastal path
from Lochranza, with an interesting
scramble over a rockfall en route, this
cave is set back from the shore with just
a small entrance you have to climb up
into and then opens out into a cosy
wee chamber – if you're lucky, complete
with night-lights.

2 DELICATESSENS

1 VALVONA & CROLLA EDIN/LOTH
19 Elm Row, Edinburgh 0131 556 6066
www.valvonacrolla.co.uk
It was my friend Lucy who introduced
me to Valvona and Crolla. When we
were students, we used to go and buy
the weirdest picnics: tiny baby
octopuses in oil, soft purple figs,
fragrant Italian sweets. We'd take them
on the bus to Portobello, tear open the
wrappings and arrive at the beach with
sticky fingers and empty bags.

I never got over the excitement of
stepping inside. As you pass through
the understated shopfront, there is
often an aria playing, a perfect
accompaniment to the high-vaulted
operatic interior and its myriad delights.
It's a temple of food with glass cases
full of gleaming cheeses, strange cured
meats hanging from the ceiling, shelves

stacked with sweets, pasta, jams, olive oils. I sometimes wander in, not to buy, just to breathe in the smells, to gaze at the vivid tomatoes and peppers. It can cure depression and fills you with a sense of the possibilities of life.

Occasionally I drink a strong coffee and sometimes buy bread, cheese and wine, but often I'm not shopping but acting in my own secret movie. Maybe others wander in, look around, breathe the smells and walk out. Maybe the staff have a name for us – but all the time I have been coming to this magical emporium, they have never failed to greet me with a warm smile. Every time is like the first time.

2 CLIVE RAMSAY'S WHLLS&T
28 Henderson Street, Bridge of Allan
01786 833 903 *www.cliveramsay.com*
Fantastic selection of exotic and intriguing foods from across the world and unique atmosphere.

3 DELIZIQUE GLAS/CLYDE
66 Hyndland Street, Glasgow
0141 339 2000 *www.delizique.co.uk*
Old-fashioned Polish deli with sausages hanging from the ceiling and friendly staff in white aprons.

4 HARVEY NICHOLS FOODHALL
EDIN/LOTH **30–34 St Andrew Square**
Edinburgh 0131 524 8388
www.harveynichols.com
Hand-made decorated chocolates, elegant cakes and bottled sauces and condiments from around the world.

5 HOUSE OF BRUAR PAD&F
Bruar, Perthshire 01796 483 236
www.houseofbruar.com
A service station so posh it doesn't even sell petrol. Great selection of quality Scottish produce.

3 BOOKSHOPS

1 THE WATERMILL PAD&F
Mill Street, Aberfeldy 01887 822 896
www.aberfeldywatermill.com
Stunning conversion of a water mill, voted Scotland's best independent bookshop in 2006, a year after it was opened by Michael Palin. The largest bookshop in rural Highlands (5,000 titles), it has an excellent children's selection. Add a top-floor art gallery, excellent range of Scottish interest books, a coffee shop, plentiful seats for casual browsers, and you'll realise why owner Kevin Ramage isn't running scared of the internet: 'If you specialise and offer something completely different, it's no threat at all.'

2 THE BOOKSHOP SOUTH SCOT
17 North Main Street, Wigtown
01988 402 499 *www.the-bookshop.com*
A bit of a presumptuous name, given that Wigtown has another 14 of them, but it IS the biggest – with over a kilometre of shelving in nine rooms – and it did get there first: when Wigtown was declared Scottish Book Town, it was the only bookshop for miles. Since Shaun Bythell took over in 2001, it has expanded to some 90,000 titles. 'These are supposed to be hard times for second-hand bookshops, but we're doing fine,' he says. 'We are building a substantial internet business. If you know what you're looking for, the internet is the thing – but if you're just browsing, there's nothing like a bookshop.'

3 WORD POWER BOOKSHOP
EDIN/LOTH **43 West Nicolson Street,**
Edinburgh 0131 662 9112
www.word-power.co.uk

fish meal for the cheapskate (but not if you're looking for a cheap skate).

4 TJ HUGHES GLAS/CLYDE
127-135 Trongate, Glasgow
0141 548 8400 *www.tjhughes.co.uk*
Proceed to the cuisinerie on the second floor of Mr Hughes's East End budget bazaar. In the afternoons, there will be purveyed, for the benefit of the jaded shop-hopper, and for £1.95, the crème de la cream tea. Request your choice of caffeine-imbued beverage and self-select the biggest, jammed and creamed scone – plain or fruit – you'll ever come across. A meal in itself. When you leave, truly will you think: scone but not forgotten.

5 CREWS CAFÉ WHLLS&T
Stirling Bus Station, 19 Goosecroft Road, Stirling 01786 473 030
This location recently celebrated its tenth anniversary and would surely top any list of Best Scottish Bus Stations. Provides the kind of food you would expect and, for £1.40, a pancake or scone with tea or coffee. It's advertised as an OAP Special but they don't ask for proof of age.

7 PLACES TO SKIM STONES

1 AUCHMITHIE PAD&F
Three miles north-east of Arbroath, Angus *(off the A92)*
www.angusahead.com
You will never get the chance to look at the scenery at Auchmithie because you will be too busy looking at the stones. Auchmithie conglomerate, the volcanic extrusion responsible for their amazing colours, produces pink stones with black

spots, green ones with yellow stripes and black stones marbled with every colour imaginable – and every third one is a skimmer. There's also a good restaurant in the village, the But 'n' Ben, where you can feast on local seafood.

2 RIVER TAY PAD&F
Dunkeld, Perthshire *(just off the A9)*
www.undiscoveredscotland.co.uk/ dunkeld/dunkeld/index.html
There is a lovely little beach on the walk upstream of Dunkeld House Hotel, beside a still pool on a gentle section of the river, surrounded by large trees. I once saw my brother-in-law skim a 17-bouncer there, and I'm not sure it's possible to do more than that – but maybe that's arguable among ace skimmers. Watch out for anglers, who might be less impressed with your fish scaring.

3 BROUGHTY FERRY PAD&F
Dundee *(off the A930)*
www.cometobroughty.co.uk
The grassy beach – located on the Firth of Tay, between Stannergate and the Royal Tay Yacht Club, off the A930 Dundee Road West – is a great spot. Searching for skimming stones is a wonderfully relaxing pastime, with the views along the Tay from here adding to it.

4 BADENSCAILLE HIGHLANDS
Achiltibuie, Wester Ross *(go west off the A835 at Drumrunie and follow a minor road round past Loch Osgaig)*
www.achiltibuie.com
A beautiful beach beside the Badenscaille burial ground on the edge of Achiltibuie, overlooking Horse Sound and the Summer Isles. A super place for

skimming stones when the tide is in. When it's out, the beach is also an idyllic spot for sandcastle building and eagle spotting.

5 CASTLE TIORAM WHLLS&T
Loch Moidart, Western Highlands *(head south from Ardmolich on the winding A861) www.moidart.org.uk*
A perfect spot for picking over stones looking for skimmers, so long as you do not get sucked into shell hunting instead. If there is no skimming to be had because of low tide, you can get across the causeway to the castle, although you can no longer go inside the 14th-century building, which has been at the centre of a long-running dispute between its owner and Historic Scotland over restoration plans.

8 FAMILY WALKS

1 DOLLAR GLEN WHLLS&T
Clackmannanshire
www.walking.visitscotland.com (search Dollar Glen)
With lush, moss-covered rocks, crystal clear pools, dramatic waterfalls and primeval-looking ferns, Dollar Glen can seem like a little piece of the tropics in Scotland. Carved deep into the Ochils, the glen rises steeply, with a well-tended path snaking towards 15th-century Castle Campbell. There are perilous-looking drops so take care with adventurous children, but for the most part, the route is suitable for anyone with a modicum of fitness, and bejewelled with places to stop for a picnic or breather.

2 JOHN MUIR COUNTRY PARK
EDIN/LOTH **Dunbar, East Lothian**
www.eastlothian.gov.uk

(search John Muir, then click on John Muir Country Park)
Spectacular walk along East Lothian coastline including remains of Dunbar Castle, Belhaven Bay and the Cliff Top Trail, with views of Bass Rock and extensive areas of saltmarsh, grassland and woodland. There's a play park at Linkfield Car Park, plus toilets, picnic tables and barbecues. Approach to the car park is from the A1 along the A1087, and is clearly signposted.

3 THE HERMITAGE PAD&F
Dunkeld 01350 728 641
Well-marked paths through beautiful Caledonian forest with some of Britain's tallest trees. At the right time of the year, there's a good chance of seeing a red squirrel and a leaping salmon. Also takes in history and mythology with Ossian's Cave (not to be confused with Ossian's Cave, Arran!).

4 GLENCORSE VIEW WALK
EDIN/LOTH **Pentlands**
www.edinburgh.gov.uk/phrp/index
Start at Flotterstone visitor centre, off the A702. Follow posts marked with a heron, along Glencorse burn to the reservoir. It's an easy walk with plenty to see: farm animals as well as wildlife. There are also hill paths from Flotterstone for fitter, more adventurous families. To reward exertion, Flotterstone Inn offers delicious pub meals.

5 GLENASHDALE FALLS SOUTH SCOT
Arran *www.ayrshire-arran.com/ itineraries/walking*
The Falls is a good walk for small feet (with snacks to keep them going and hide-and-seek coming back). Take the left bank of the river for a prettier

route through the forest and a better view at the top, but prepare for a final steep slog.

9 ICE CREAM

1 JANNETTAS PAD&F
31 South Street, St Andrews, Fife 01334 473 285 www.jannettas.co.uk
A perfect way to complete a walk around St Andrews Cathedral or along the pier is to stop at Jannettas and enjoy one of their 52 flavours of ice-cream. A favourite with students in the university town since it opened in 1908. The mint choc chip is fantastic but the Scottish tablet, Turkish delight and Irn-Bru sorbet all pull in the crowds too.

2 S LUCA EDIN/LOTH
32–38 High Street, Musselburgh 0131 665 2237 and 10 Morningside Road, Edinburgh 0131 446 0233 www.s-luca.co.uk
The selection of flavours may not match the might of Baskin-Robbins or Ben & Jerry's, but the quality takes some licking. Over the years S Luca has become a byword for authentic Italian ice-cream. Just don't expect to get a tub or cone right away if your visit coincides with anything resembling a heatwave. Luca's takeaway queue is almost as legendary as its ice-cream.

3 ALLANWATER CAFÉ WHLLS&T
15 Henderson Street, Bridge of Allan 01786 833 060 www.bridgeofallan.org
The Allanwater has recently introduced new flavours on to the menu, but the vanilla ice-cream served up there remains the best I've ever tasted. The recipe has been a fiercely-guarded secret since the café was founded in 1902, and in the summer the locals queue out of the door to stock up.

4 CORRIERI'S WHLLS&T
9 Alloa Road, Stirling 01786 472 089
Not only is it in a great location, at the foot of the Wallace Monument in Stirling, but this place's home-made Italian ice-cream prompts visitors to make long trips from Glasgow, Edinburgh and elsewhere. It can't hurt it that it is situated right alongside one of the best children's playparks in the country with a boating and paddling pool in the centre. On a sunny day, it is without doubt the perfect place to enjoy your double oyster.

5 EQUI'S GLAS/CLYDE
Burnbank Road, Hamilton 01698 282 494 www.equi.demon.co.uk
This North Lanarkshire institution was established in 1922 and, although nowhere near a beach, customers know they can recapture that holiday feeling every day of the year. For three generations, Equi ice-cream makers have honed the traditional homemade Scottish milk and double cream recipe, available in family favourites – including double cream vanilla – and newer flavours, such as Surfing the Nut. People come from across Scotland for this ice-cream, but if you want a sweet treat without cream, try the amazing sorbets – mango or vodka and Red Bull.

10 SANDWICH BARS

1 QUPI EDIN/LOTH
171 Leith Walk, Edinburgh 0131 555 2900
Its fresh and innovative (not to mention

addictive) baguettes, salads and croques in a laid-back atmosphere keep it bustling all day long. Its comfy sofas are perfect for lounging with latte and a newspaper.

2 PAUL'S ORIGINAL SANDWICH HOUSE (POSH) EDIN/LOTH
103 Hanover Street, Edinburgh
0131 624 6633
The sandwiches are quite favourably priced, depending on which type of bread you prefer, and they're not skimpy on filling either. Deep-filled clubs are excellent, and it's not a problem having anything toasted while you take a seat (very few around at lunchtime, mind).

3 SUBWAY (everywhere)
www.subway.com
£1.99 for Sub of the Day is a bargain and, with no butter or mayo, healthier than many prepacked sandwiches. You can choose your own bread type, salad filling and sauces, and even have it toasted. Some city branches are open virtually 24 hours, offering a guilt-free option to late-night takeaways.

4 FILLING STATION EDIN/LOTH
18a Kitchener Cres, Longniddry
01875 853 525
Great value for money – fresh rolls, baguettes, rolls, cakes, every topping under the sun, run by a great team of five or six women. It opens very, very early and you can even eat there before going to bed after a long night out. All freshly cooked or made in front of you – none of that prepacked nonsense – with a plethora of bonus toppings that are included in the price. It all takes place in a very small wooden hut across the road from the station with a

few seats outside. Glorious smells travel all across the village.

5 SCRUMPTIOUS PAD&F
156 High Street, Auchterarder
01764 664 430
All was not lost when its namesake coffee shop in Crieff closed: the Manx-Australian owners kept on their takeaway in Auchterarder. Quality ingredients and a few idiosyncrasies along the way.

11 MUNROS FOR NOVICES

1 BEN LOMOND (3,195 ft) WHLLS&T
You won't be lonely on this one: it's the southernmost Munro and one of the most popular. An obvious path leads through varied terrain of woods, grassy slopes and a stony upper section. The final approach to the summit is along a dramatic, though non-scary, ridge with fantastic views across Loch Lomond to the mountains of Arrochar and beyond. Very accessible for Central Belt dwellers. Start: Rowardennan car park at end of the road up the eastern side of Loch Lomond.

2 BEN CHONZIE (3,054 ft) PAD&F
An undemanding walk, and very difficult to get lost. Make fast progress up a track that takes you much of the way to the top, then follow a fence for the final stage. The summit is something of a plateau, and were it not for the cairn you would be doubtful which was the highest point. If tackling this one in winter, look out for Arctic hares. Start: Invergeldie, near Comrie, Perthshire.

3 THE CAIRNWELL (3,061 ft)
HIGHLANDS
A dawdle, or the nearest you can get to

one while bagging a Munro. Ski-tow paraphernalia is a bit of an eyesore, but also an aid to navigation. Heathery slopes nearly all the way. On the summit, if you still feel energetic, contemplate bagging the neighbours Carn Aosda (3,008 ft) and Carn a'Gheoid (3,199 ft) too. Start: Glenshee Ski Centre.

4 BEINN GHLAS *(3,619 ft)* WHLLS&T
Don't be deterred by the height: your starting point is 1,476 ft. Straight-forward and well-frequented route, with springy turf to walk on and birds such as wheatear, ring-ouzel and ptarmigan. On the summit, if all has gone like a dream and you're up for more exertion, the ninth-highest Munro, Ben Lawers (3,983 ft), is within reach. Tea and cakes in the visitor centre café will be your reward. Start: Ben Lawers Visitor Centre, north-west of Loch Tay.

5 SCHIEHALLION *(3,553 ft)* PAD&F
A substantial hill, with a dramatic, conical shape but nothing to alarm beginners, and the climb repays the effort with great views in all directions. History buffs, take note: it was on these slopes that an early attempt was made to calculate the Earth's mass. Start: Braes of Foss car park, near Kinloch Rannoch.

More info: walking.visitscotland.com/munros

12 PLAYPARKS

1 THE MEADOWS EDIN/LOTH
Edinburgh
Playparks tend to consist of a few predictable attractions – swings, slide, roundabout, perhaps a climbing frame and a couple of benches for grown-ups. Not this one, at the Sciennes edge of the Meadows. A great deal of municipal thought and money (£400,000) was poured into the project. Borders artist Jeremy Cunningham was brought in to sculpt and landscape; even the kids were consulted. The result is superb, with a mechanical watery thing (an Archimedes Screw), pedal-power roundabout, flying fox, big climbing rock and much more.

2 CASTLE GREEN PAD&F
Broughty Ferry *and* **CAMPERDOWN PARK, Dundee** *www.dundeecity.gov.uk*
Castle Green must be one of Scotland's most dramatically sited playparks. Virtually in the shadow of Broughty Castle, it also affords commanding views of the coastal sweep of Dundee as it banks up the hillside from the Tay. The play equipment ranges from extensive climbing frames for different ages to an inventive series of pulleys, conveyor belts and diggers. In the summer, an added attraction is the large soft play surface dotted with water-spouts, showers and fountains which switch on and off intermittently to the delight of soon-to-be-soaked youngsters.

However, the playpark is dwarfed by the sheer scale of an amazing play complex hidden deep in Camperdown Park, at the other (western) end of Dundee. A series of brightly coloured enclosures aimed at different age groups stretches as far as the eye can see, featuring everything from castles to pirate ships, along with ramps for just-mobile tots to rope swings irresistible to dads.

3 FINLAYSTONE ESTATE GLAS/CLYDE
near Langbank, Renfrewshire
www.finlaystonehouse.com
This is a fantastic woodland play area,
including wooden forts, ships and
wigwams to clamber about in, in a
delightful setting.

4 BOTANIC GARDENS GLAS/CLYDE
Glasgow *www.glasgow.gov.uk*
Popular with West Enders, it has slides,
climbing frames and roundabouts,
providing toddler heaven inside the
verdant oasis of the Botanics.

5 VOGRIE COUNTRY PARK
EDIN/LOTH **near Gorebridge, Midlothian**
www.midlothian.gov.uk
A brilliant adventure play area inside a
brilliant country park. Keeps kids of all
ages occupied for hours with great
swings that look like they are going to
bash into each other but never do, a
fast twister of a slide down the hill, a
death slide and a huge spider's web.

6 VICTORIA PARK EDIN/LOTH
Trinity, Edinburgh *www.edinburgh.*
gov.uk/internet/Leisure
A superb and very different modern
playpark with a hugely innovative
design. Lots of fun for a broad age
range – including adults.

13 ITALIAN RESTAURANTS

1 ESCA GLAS/CLYDE
27 Chisholm Street, Glasgow
0141 553 0880 *www.esca.5pm.co.uk*
Hidden across from the Tron theatre, a
tiny restaurant which blends Italian and
wider Mediterranean cuisine with first-
class service and a very personal touch.
From intimate dinners for two to a girls'

night out or family celebrations, the
staff take great care of you. And the
food... melt-in-the-mouth, generous
portions with the right flashes of
innovation. Marvellous desserts. The
lunch and pre-theatre set menus are
very well-priced and offer the variety of
choice so lacking in the set menus of
rivals.

2 VITTORIA'S EDIN/LOTH
113 Brunswick Street, Edinburgh
0131 556 6171 *and* **19 George IV Bridge,**
Edinburgh 0131 225 1740
www.vittoriarestaurant.com
This big, family-run restaurant is
something of an institution, with its
huge menu catering for all tastes,
whether they claim to enjoy Italian
food or not. The pasta is always freshly
cooked and there are some great Italian
ice-creams to finish off. Despite the size
of the place, booking is normally
essential.

3 SARTI GLAS/CLYDE
133 Wellington St, Glasgow
0141 248 2228 *www.sarti.co.uk*
There are three Sartis in town (the
others are at 121 Bath Street and 42
Renfield Street), but the best is the
original in Wellington Street. The food
really is an authentic slice of Italian
cooking. Ingredients are imported
direct from Italy and the restaurant is
crowded, intimate and welcoming to
children.

4 CARMINE'S PASTA & PIZZA
ABER/GRAMP **32 Union Terrace,**
Aberdeen 01224 624 145
The man regulars call Carmine might
seem to have opened his restaurant as
far away from sunny Southern Italy as
he could imagine, but keeps its flavours

alive with his cooking and a constant soundtrack of opera. Stars appearing at His Majesty's Theatre (across the road) have been known to join the queue.

5 BELLA ITALIA EDIN/LOTH
12 High Street, North Berwick, East Lothian 01620 893 916
Been going for 25 years and has maintained the standard for all those years. Fantastic place with a great range of food.

14 TRADITIONAL MUSIC VENUES

1 SANDY BELL'S BAR EDIN/LOTH
25 Forrest Road, Edinburgh 0131 225 2751
The revival in traditional music and song means it's easier than ever before to hear it – either in informal pub sessions where it flourishes or in the concert hall. The session scene can change almost from week to week, but among a few dependable venues, in Edinburgh you can expect a cluster of fiddlers or other instrumentalists round a table any night of the week in the famed Sandy Bell's. Good crack – but expect things to be cramped when busy.

2 BABBITY BOWSTER GLAS/CLYDE
16-18 Blackfriars Street, Glasgow 0141 552 5055
In the heart of Glasgow's Merchant City, this convivial cross between urban bistro and folk howff hosts Saturday afternoon singing and playing sessions. Good beer and good food, too.

3 HOOTANANNY HIGHLANDS
67 Church Street, Inverness 01463 233 651 www.hootananny.co.uk
This award-winning venue boasts folk music every night of the week, from casual tune sessions to 'name' guests.

4 ROYAL OAK EDIN/LOTH
1 Infirmary Street, Edinburgh 0131 557 2976 www.royal-oak-folk.com
Regular, intimate folk and blues sessions and weekly gatherings of its advisedly named Wee Folk Club.

15 ROBERT BURNS SITES

1 BURNS HOUSE SOUTH SCOT
Burns St, Dumfries 01387 255 297 www.burnsscotland.com/tours/dumfries
It was in this ordinary sandstone building that Burns spent the last years of his life. Now a place of pilgrimage for enthusiasts from around the world, the house retains much of its 18th-century character and contains many relics of the poet. There is the chair in which he wrote his last poems, many original letters and manuscripts, and the famous Kilmarnock and Edinburgh editions of his work.

2 BURNS HERITAGE PARK
SOUTH SCOT Murdoch's Lone, Alloway, Ayr 01292 443 700 www.burnsheritagepark.com
Burns's birthplace is brought to life through a mixture of modern technology and unique, authentic locations and artefacts. Travel back in time in Robert Burns Cottage and visit the Burns family. See the world's most important Robert Burns collection in the museum.

3 THE GLOBE INN SOUTH SCOT
56 High St, Dumfries 01387 252 335
Established in 1610, the Globe has long been associated with Burns. In 1796, he

wrote: 'The Globe Tavern here, which these many years has been my Howff…', and first held a Burns Supper way back in 1819. At his howff (haunt), packed with memorabilia, his favourite seat still survives and some of his poetry may still be seen, inscribed by Burns on his bedroom windows.

4 BURNS HERMITAGE SOUTH SCOT
near Friars Carse Hotel, Auldgirth, Dumfries 01387 740 388
www.friarscarse.co.uk
Once the family home of Captain Riddell, a friend and patron of Burns, this handsome country house is now a hotel. It is surrounded by beautiful woodland, in which is hidden the building known as Burns Hermitage. Burns came here, to what he referred to as the 'ivied cot', to talk with his friends at Friars Carse and to write poetry, for these years were some of the most fruitful of his life.

5 ELLISLAND FARM SOUTH SCOT
Auldgirth, Dumfriesshire
www.ellislandfarm.co.uk
Here, at this attractive listed steading, Burns wrote many of his most famous poems, including 'Tam o'Shanter' and 'Auld Lang Syne'. An audio-visual display tells the story of his life.

16 REAL CIDER PUBS

1 THE THREE JUDGES GLAS/CLYDE
141 Dumbarton Road, Glasgow
0141 337 3055
The best pub for cider lovers. A truly traditional Glasgow pub in the West End that regularly holds cask cider festivals with an inspiring range,

including Thatcher's Farmers Tipple and Mole's Black Rat Cider. Its festivals usually last for two weeks – plenty of time to make your way through the selection. It has a good range of UK ciders on tap, including Heck's Dry. It also does a brilliant home-made pork pie – perfect with your pint.

2 THE CLOCKWORK BEER CO
GLAS/CLYDE
1153–1155 Cathcart Road, Glasgow
0141 649 0184 *www.maclay.com*
In Glasgow's Southside, the Clockwork is a spacious, split-level bar where you can always get good chat and a great pint. It is well-known for having its own micro-brewery and has Weston's Vintage on tap. Always a great atmosphere, especially on match days as it is close to Hampden. Recently voted the best pub for watching football in the west of Scotland by Tennent's customers.

3 THE SOUTHSIDER EDIN/LOTH
3–7 West Richmond Street, Edinburgh
0131 667 2003
A lively pub in Edinburgh to enjoy a pint of Addlestone's Cloudy cider. There's always a really good mix of people. A recent refurbishment has given it a new lease of life. The Wednesday quiz is hugely popular and there is live music on Saturdays – always a good night.

4 CASK AND BARREL EDIN/LOTH
115 Broughton Street, Edinburgh
0131 556 3132
This pub has a really welcoming feel – it's very traditional with its horseshoe bar and dark, wooden decor. It has a really nice atmosphere and is worth a visit to sample the range of ciders. It

has tables outside in the summer, so you can have a pint and make the most of the rare sunshine.

5 MALT AND HOPS EDIN/LOTH
45 The Shore, Edinburgh 0131 555 0083
A traditional pub overlooking the water at Leith. The cask-conditioned cider is not for the faint-hearted. It's a real old-fashioned place, decorated with beer mats and mirrors. The roaring fire makes this the perfect place to spend a winter night – the cider will warm you up.

17 WINTER YOUTH HOSTELS

1 AVIEMORE YOUTH HOSTEL
HIGHLANDS **25 Grampian Rd, Aviemore 01479 810 345**
Aviemore is an undisputed contender for the winter sports capital of Scotland. The town offers easy access to a dazzling array of winter activities, such as skiing, snowboarding and winter mountaineering. When the snow falls, there are few better places to be in Scotland. The hostel is five minutes' walk from the town centre and offers a great base for all the action.

2 EDINBURGH CENTRAL YOUTH HOSTEL EDIN/LOTH
9 Haddington Place, Edinburgh 0131 524 2090
When the darkness of winter falls, Edinburgh lights up into a veritable winter wonderland, with plenty of festive fun to be had in the city centre and beyond. The SYHA's flagship five-star hostel in Leith Walk is within easy reach of Princes Street and the shops, and allows you to buy Christmas presents without breaking the bank.

3 GLASGOW YOUTH HOSTEL
GLAS/CLYDE **8 Park Terrace, Glasgow 0141 332 3004**
If shopping is what you are looking for this Christmas, you need go no further than Glasgow, where shoppers pack the streets of elegant Buchanan Street looking for festive gifts. The hostel, conveniently located between the city centre and the West End, allows you to escape from the bustle at night to a relaxing oasis in one of the most vibrant parts of the city.

4 ABERDEEN YOUTH HOSTEL
ABER/GRAMP **8 Queen's Road, Aberdeen 01224 646 988**
The Granite City has its own thriving winter spirit and the vibes on busy Union Street as Christmas approaches are always good. Aberdeen's festive lights are second to none and the cold wind off the North Sea makes the shops even more inviting. The hostel lies an easy 15-minute walk from the city's heart.

5 OBAN YOUTH HOSTEL WHLLS&T
Esplanade, Oban 01631 562 025
Our islands are often overlooked in winter, but the colder months can be a great time to hop on the ferry. The winter light of the west coast has a more beautiful quality than any you will ever see. This is a great place to start the trip.

Details at www.syha.org.uk

18 FREE THINGS TO DO WITH CHILDREN

1 FLYING KITES ON THE WEST SANDS BEACH AT ST ANDREWS
PAD&F **Kingdom of Fife Tourist Board
0845 2255 121** *www.standrews.co.uk*
There is always a breeze on the beach at St Andrews, so most children's kites will fly. There is also plenty of room to run around, a Sunday morning is quiet and a free car park is located beside the beach. If you have no kite, pretend you are in *Chariots of Fire* and run along the beach. There are also interesting rock pools to have a look in.

2 CAMPERDOWN PARK PAD&F
**Coupar Angus Road, Dundee
01382 431 818**
www.camperdownpark.com
Camperdown has a huge play area with loads of play equipment on sand. It is in stages, so you move from one area to another, then back again. The park is also good for riding bikes, walking and flying kites.

3 WALKING THE FORTH ROAD BRIDGE EDIN/LOTH
Forth Bridges Visitor Centre Trust
www.forthbridges.org.uk
Fantastic fun, looking at the islands below, the trains going over the rail bridge, or just watching the boats on the Forth. It is a great sight to see the Superfast ferry leave Rosyth and go under both bridges.

4 CYCLING ALONG THE WATER OF LEITH EDIN/LOTH **Water of Leith Visitor Centre, Lanark Road, Edinburgh**

0131 455 7367 *or* **0131 443 1682**
www.waterofleith.org.uk
The path from Slateford to Balerno is lovely, it is a very gentle incline and very safe, but beware the dog-walkers. Lots of places just to stop and look at the water and have a rest. Coming back, you pick up a bit of speed, which is fun and just right for children to really enjoy. If you want a snack, Juniper Green has some great small shops and pubs.

5 AN AFTERNOON AT YELLOW-CRAIG BEACH EDIN/LOTH
Dirleton, near North Berwick, East Lothian
The park at Yellowcraig (turn off the main road into Dirleton then follow the signs to the beach) is great fun for kids of all ages and adults alike. There is a huge swinging tyre, brilliant climbing ropes and enough variety to keep the children busy for ages. Afterwards, walk down to the beach, a fabulous long stretch of gorgeous sand with superb views across the Forth. It is great for paddling in the warmer weather – and for walking dogs, building sandcastles and playing games any time. If you feel adventurous, head along to North Berwick for some fish and chips.

19 PLACES TO SEE OWLS

There are four species of owl regularly recorded in Scotland – short-eared, long-eared, tawny and barn. Three other species – little owl, snowy owl and eagle owl – appear sporadically. Early winter is an ideal time to search for owls because of the absence of leaves on trees.

1 CAERLAVEROCK SOUTH SCOT
Dumfries and Galloway, *Ordnance Survey grid reference NY043659*
01387 770 200 *www.wwt.org.uk*
The 5,500-hectare National Nature Reserve at Caerlaverock may be more renowned to most of us for the winter spectacle of pink-footed geese, barnacle geese and whooper swan. However the multitude of observation hides over-looking salt marsh and flooded pasture provide excellent vantage points for searching for the most common owl to hunt in the daylight: the short-eared owl.

2 FALLS OF CLYDE WILDLIFE RESERVE GLAS/CLYDE
Lanarkshire, *Grid Ref NS 882 425*
01555 665 262 *www.swt.org.uk*
The tawny owl is primarily a bird of the woodland but, in recent years, has adapted to life in parks and gardens. Surprisingly difficult to see – the characteristic 'too-whit' calls are more easily heard after dusk. During the summer, the Falls of Clyde visitor centre offers 'dusk safaris', ranger-led guided walks with the chance of seeing some of the reserve's nocturnal inhabitants, including tawny owls.

3 SANDS OF FORVIE NATIONAL NATURE RESERVE ABER/GRAMP
Grid Ref NK039289 **01358 751 330**
www.nnr-scotland.org.uk
The Sands of Forvie National Nature Reserve is a huge area of sand dunes and coastal heath on the Ythan Estuary, 12 miles north of Aberdeen. Long-eared owls can be seen hunting in the fields and salt marsh near the car park at Waterside Bridge. There is a visitor centre (open April–October) and a series of waymarked trails.

4 WOOD OF CREE SOUTH SCOT
Dumfries and Galloway, *Grid Ref NX381708* **01556 670 464**
www.rspb.org.uk
The floodplain marshes, willow carr and field margins of the Wood of Cree are ideal hunting grounds for barn owls. Over the past 50 years, barn owls have suffered catastrophic declines as a result of the degradation of agricultural habitats, but thankfully this decline has been halted in recent years and the population in Scotland may now be increasing once more.

5 ISLE OF LEWIS OUT. ISLES
Stornoway Tourist Information Centre
01851 703 088
www.thewesternisles.co.uk
For the past couple of years, the Isle of Lewis has witnessed the winter arrival of between two and six snowy owls. These birds, more at home in the open tundra of the Arctic Circle, have ventured south to the northern tip of Lewis. Instead of lemmings, snowy owls in Scotland switch to feeding on rabbits and voles. Anyone fortunate enough to witness snowy owls in the windswept coastal dunes of Lewis truly has been witness to one of Scotland's most surreal wildlife spectacles.

20 BROCHS

1 MIDHOWE BROCH OUT. ISLES
Rousay, Orkney
www.undiscoveredscotland.co.uk/ rousay/midhowebroch/index.html
Situated on the small island of Rousay to the north of Orkney mainland, with a beautiful position overlooking Eynhallow Sound. One of the earliest brochs in Orkney, it has been suggested

that it simply served as a fortified family home rather than as part of a larger domestic complex. It was first occupied in the second century BC but now finds itself having to be defended from the ravages of the sea.

2 DUN CARLOWAY OUT. ISLES
Carloway, Stornoway, Lewis
www.undiscoveredscotland.co.uk
Lying on the west coast of Lewis, overlooking Loch Roag, this well-preserved broch is the best example of its kind in the Western Isles. Its position atop a rocky mound and wall remnants up to nine metres high give a real sense of what an imposing structure it must have seemed more than 2,000 years ago. It has an excellent wee visitor centre that helps to interpret the ruins.

3 GLENELG BROCHS HIGHLANDS
Near Glenelg, Kintail
www.lochalsh.co.uk
Located in a small glen to the south of Glenelg village, this complex consists of a pair of brochs, Dun Telve and Dun Trodden, with another broch some two miles up the glen. Dun Telve is the best-preserved broch on the Scottish mainland, with walls 10m high in parts. It may be the work of itinerant broch builders from Skye, but folklore suggests it was the home of the Scottish giant Fingal.

4 BROCH OF GURNESS OUT. ISLES
Aikerness, Orkney *www.historic-scot-land.gov.uk (search Gurness)*
Located on mainland Orkney, this is one of Scotland's most majestic brochs. It has three fortified ramparts that enclose an array of Iron Age domestic buildings that may have been home to over 30 families. It remained in use for

more than 1,000 years; later, it was the home of a Viking iron foundry. The ruins at Gurness are a match for those of nearby Skara Brae and Maes Howe.

5 MOUSA BROCH OUT. ISLES
Island of Mousa, Shetland *(accessible by boat from Sandwick, about 14m South of Lerwick on the A970. For ferry contact operator, telephone* **01950 431 367.** *More info:* **01856 841 815)**
Rising to a height of 14m, this is the best-preserved broch in Scotland. It is to be found on Mousa, one of the smaller islands in Shetland and is unusual in that it lacks a complex of surrounding buildings. There is some suggestion that it marks some kind of end-stage in broch building in Scotland where defence rather than status became the order of the day. It is mentioned in the Norse sagas of Orkney and Shetland.

21 DIVE SITES

1 ST CATHERINE'S WHLLS&T
Loch Fyne
This is a great site when learning to dive; the visibility can be good and is great for compass work and tests. There are squat lobsters and starfish to see and lots of crabs, which can make it a fun dive.

2 BASS ROCK EDIN/LOTH
North Berwick, East Lothian
This is a good dive site if you want to see lobsters, and big ones at that.

3 GREEN GULLY SOUTH SCOT
Eyemouth, Berwickshire
This is another of Scotland's hidden treasures – there is a very steep climb down to the water and a real killer of a climb back up, but is well worth a go

warblers, redstarts and pied flycatchers, with the chance of seeing grasshopper warblers near the Cree river. Greater spotted and green woodpeckers drum on trees and bullfinch and long-tailed tits are visible in the tree tops. Nuthatches have also moved into this part of southern Scotland, and tree creepers and jays can also be watched.

24 BUTCHERS

1 CHARLES MACLEOD HIGHLANDS
Family Butchers, Stornoway, Isle of Lewis 01851 702 445
www.charlesmacleod.co.uk
This is the place that makes the famed Stornoway black pudding that appears on Michelin-starred restaurant menus across Europe. Known locally as Charley Barley's, it's huge inside with plenty of high-quality, fresh local meat for sale. As well as their ubiquitous black pudding, or *marag dubh*, to use the Gaelic, they also do a white and a fruit pudding, and the friendly staff will make recommendations based on exactly what you're after. For those who can't make the trek, they also sell online.

2 DUNCAN FRASER HIGHLANDS
Queensgate, Inverness 01463 233 066
www.duncanfraserbutcher.co.uk
A member of the Q-Guild of butchers and among the very best in the UK. The traditional Ayrshire recipe bacon is delicious and the beef is exceptional – a trip to their shop is a must.

3 A F CUTHILL EDIN/LOTH
60 Warrender Park Road, Edinburgh 0131 229 2986
Terrific meat from people who take pride in selling top-quality produce.

Owned by Frank Duns, who has worked at the family business for more than 30 years. Lamb and beef particularly good. A treasure.

4 BALAGOWAN WHLLS&T
Glen Lean, Dunoon 01369 705 319
www.winstonchurchillvenison.com
Winston Churchill not only handles the packing and processing of meat but stalks and shoots it too. The former gamekeeper (yes, it is his real name) has embraced every process from field to plate. Customers can even book an excursion with deerstalkers to get the meat. The company hangs, processes, packages and dispatches venison and pheasants to local outlets such as the Loch Fyne Oyster Bar or via mail order. Venison is very low in cholesterol and fat and tastes fantastic.

5 GEORGE BOWER EDIN/LOTH
75 Raeburn Place, Edinburgh 0131 332 3469
Unplucked pheasants hanging from tiled walls, fresh rabbit, venison or pigeon breasts behind the counter and beef in the window. Bower's is heaven for meat-lovers and the 40-minute turkey queue is a Christmas ritual.

25 WILD PLACES

1 ST ABB'S HEAD SOUTH SCOT
OS Landranger 47, Duns, Dunbar and Eyemouth, *Grid Ref 913691*
South of Dunbar, St Abb's Head is owned by the National Trust for Scotland and is formed from an extinct volcano. Arrive by public transport or park at the visitors' car park and make your way up to the rugged headland to the viewpoint and lighthouse and be blown away – not literally – by the fantastic

cliffs and gullies and stacks, made all the more dramatic in the wild weather.

2 ARDNAMURCHAN POINT

HIGHLANDS **OS Landranger 47, Tobermory and North East Mull**
Grid Ref 416 674
Most westerly point on mainland Britain, and a long drive to get there on winding, single-track roads but, on a wild day, the enormous seas breaking over the rocks and lighthouse can be truly amazing. If the weather is clear, you'll be able to see the white spray of waves against the islands of Eigg, Rum and Muck as well.

3 NEIST POINT HIGHLANDS

OS Landranger 23, North Skye
Grid Ref 128463
The most westerly point on Skye: Neist Point has one of the most dramatic landscapes in Scotland and one of the most interesting little footpaths to get there, being the only access to the lighthouse and overlooked by the looming Moonan Bay. Once out at the point, you find a shattered pavement of rock where hours can be spent scrambling about.

4 RHUE LIGHTHOUSE HIGHLANDS

OS Landranger 19, Gairloch and Ullapool, *Grid Ref 092975, (north of Ullapool)*
Easy to get to by taking the road north from Ullapool and turning off on to the single-track road to Rhue, park at the car park and walk down to the lighthouse that almost teeters over the edge of the sea cliffs. The sea here can be a wonderful green, even on the wildest of days and there's the possibility of seeing the seals that live around Loch Broom.

5 SANDWOOD BAY HIGHLANDS

OS Landranger 9, Cape Wrath
Grid Ref 220652, **Sutherland**
Leave the road at Blairmore near Kinlochbervie, then it's four miles of easy walking to a bay that has everything: Am Buachaille (the Shepherd), an impressive sea stack; a long, sandy beach; cliffs and a ruin.

26 FARM SHOPS/ FARMERS' MARKETS

1 GLOAGBURN FARM PAD&F

Tibbermore, Perth 01738 840 864
www.gloagburnfarmshop.co.uk
On the outskirts of Perth, Gloagburn serves superb food: its crab and lime tart is especially delicious, as are the out-of-the-ordinary soups and home-baking. Small wonder the queues stretch as far as the duckpond.

2 JAMESFIELD ORGANIC CENTRE

PAD&F **Jamesfield Farm, Abernethy 01738 850 498**
www.jamesfieldfarm.co.uk
Another super place, with a comprehensive organic shop and a lovely restaurant with views over the farm's sprawling 300 acres. A much larger restaurant than Gloagburn, it also serves high-quality food in a farmyard setting (more coos and ducks). Has online ordering service.

3 LOCH LEVEN'S LARDER PAD&F

Channel Farm, Milnathort, Kinross 01592 841 000
www.lochlevenslarder.com
The larder is personally run by the farmer's wife. Lunches are first-class again, using the farm's produce. Always

busy. No duckpond however, but lots of animals in the fields which lead down to the loch! If you are the type to sway with ecstasy when beholding designer chutneys and cheeses, it is browsing heaven. Very child-friendly with an outdoor play area and pigs and goats to pet. Also offers stunning panoramic views over Loch Leven.

4 CRAIGIE'S FARM DELI AND CAFÉ
EDIN/LOTH **West Craigie Farm, South Queensferry, 0131 319 1048**
www.craigies.co.uk
Just off the A90 near Dalmeny, Craigie Farm has been in existence as a farm shop for some years. The farmer/owner has recently built a brand-new shop and café: again, excellent food beautifully put together.

5 THE COFFEE BOTHY WHLLS&T
Blairmains Farm Shop, Blairlogie, Stirling 01259 762 266
www.blairmainsfarmshop.co.uk
Just east of Stirling, off the Alloa road, the Coffee Bothy has excellent salads, interesting soups and scrumptious cakes, all made on the premises. Well worth the detour off the main road.

6 FARMERS' MARKET EDIN/LOTH
Castle Terrace, Edinburgh
www.edinburghcc.com
Large, high-quality market attracts healthy crowds on Saturdays. Lots of fun tastings. Open from 9am to 2pm.

7 FENTON BARNS EDIN/LOTH
**North Berwick, East Lothian
01620 850 202**
Part of an interesting rural complex with a wide range of quality local produce.

8 LOCH FYNE OYSTER BAR
WHLLS&T **Cairndow, Argyll
01499 600 264 *www.lochfyne.com***
There are plenty of seafood goodies to be had from the famous Argyll eatery's comprehensive larder. And, on the last Saturday of every month, it hosts its own farmers' market. So, if you don't have time to stop for a meal, why not pick up some fresh mussels or a lovely Loch Fyne kipper or two the next time you're passing?

27 INDEPENDENT WINE SHOPS

1 WINES AT 39 EDIN/LOTH
**39a Queen Street, Edinburgh
0131 220 6889 *www.winesat39.com***
Stocks a range of French wines and champagne, most imported from small vineyards which Joe McHugh, the owner, has spent many years visiting. Joe ditched his IT career to open the shop and is a passionate wine enthusiast, always keen to share his tips and recommendations with his customers at informal tastings in the shop.

2 LOCKETT BROS WINE & WHISKY SPECIALISTS EDIN/LOTH
**133 High Street, North Berwick
01620 890 799 *www.lockettbros.co.uk***
Journey along the East Lothian coastline to discover this hidden gem. The shelves are peppered with interesting wines and cult vintages from growers all over the world. It is fast establishing itself as a strong independent wine merchant that oozes passion and enthusiasm.

3 WOODWINTERS WINES AND WHISKIES WHLLS&T
16 Henderson Street, Bridge of Allan
01786 834 894 *www.woodwinters.com*
Recently scooping the Scottish Wine Merchant of the Year title for the second year running, WoodWinters really knows its stuff, offering dynamic wine from around the world. The shop is set out by style and variety rather than by countries and regions and has entertaining wines from £4 to £400. The business was set up by Douglas and Cara Wood, with the ethos that everyone should be able to enjoy exciting wines that are a cut above those available in the supermarket.

4 MARKINCH WINE GALLERY
PAD&F 61 High Street, Glenrothes
01592 750 024
Run by Sandy Stewart, the gallery has been serving fine wines to Fifers for more than two decades. The secret of their success has been to move with the times to reflect great improvements in winemaking and take advantage of new areas of wine production. Cheerful, friendly service is paired with wines to suit every price bracket.

5 CORNELIUS BEER & WINE
EDIN/LOTH 18 Easter Road, Edinburgh
0131 652 2405
Easter Road may not sound the most obvious location for a dynamic independent wine shop but Cornelius is an established part of the thriving community at the top end. It has a decent range of well-priced wines with a slight emphasis on the European, including some interesting Italians and a fistful of rioja. There is usually a bottle or two open for tasting on a Saturday afternoon. The staff know their stuff and if you are spending a fiver or so, you are guaranteed to be going home with a good bottle.

28 GLASSHOUSES

1 GLASSHOUSE EXPERIENCE
EDIN/LOTH Royal Botanic Gardens, Inverleith Row, Edinburgh
0131 552 7171 *www.rbge.org.uk. Open daily from 10am (not 25 Dec or 1 Jan), closes 4pm Nov–Feb, 5pm March and October, 7pm April–Sept, glasshouses close 3.30pm Nov–Feb, 5pm March–Oct*
This is an extensive range of glasshouses in Edinburgh's Royal Botanic Garden. Ten zones contain plants from all around the world. There are exotic orchids; all sorts of tropical fruit and food plants; 200-year-old cycads (so-called fossil plants, which grew when dinosaurs ruled the earth); roof-brushing palms in Britain's tallest palm house and massive bamboos. In the heat and the jungly lushness of the Tropical Aquatics House, the giant water lily *Victoria amazonica*, grown each year from a pea-sized seed, spreads its 6 ft leaves over the pond. And that hardly begins to describe it all.

2 WINTER GARDENS ABER/GRAMP
Duthie Park, Polmuir Road, Aberdeen
01224 523 201
www.aberdeencity.gov.uk Open 9.30am–6.30pm in the summer and 9.30am–3.30pm winter.
Opened in Duthie Park in 1970 to replace a gale-damaged structure, with many additions in the years since. Highlights include the seasonally changed and prodigiously colourful Victorian Corridor; one of Britain's largest collections of cacti and

succulents; the Tropical House, with orchids, ground cover of bromeliads and overhead bougainvilleas. Features plants introduced by Aberdeen-born plant collector Francis Masson, who discovered more than 1,700 species. Children will love the terrapins – but take heed of the warning notices, they bite! This is also an extremely popular wedding venue. Best of all, the Winter Gardens are free.

3 KIBBLE PALACE GLAS/CLYDE
730 Great Western Road, Glasgow 0141 276 1614 *www.glasgow.gov.uk glasshouses open 10am–4.45pm (4.15pm in winter)*
Built by James Kibble at his residence at Coulport, Loch Long, and gifted to Glasgow Botanic Gardens in 1871 as the Kibble Crystal Art Palace and Royal Conservatory. The great and graceful dome looks splendidly pristine following reopening last year after £8m dismantling and restoration. Contains a collection of Australasian tree ferns, many of which have grown there for 120 years, along with 19th-century marble sculptures.

4 ASCOG HALL FERNERY WHLLS&T
Ascog, Isle Of Bute 01700 504 555 *www.ascoghallfernery.co.uk open from Easter–end of October (closed Monday and Tuesday)*
Grotto-like sunken fernhouse, with stream and waterfall, restored in 1997. More than 100 sub-tropical ferns, corresponding to an 1879 inventory, thrive without heating due to Bute's mild climate and the underground location. One original specimen survives, with a rhizome 3 ft in diameter and 9 ft high, and is reputed to be more than 1,000 years old. A must

for the pteridophilist, this gem will turn many more into fern lovers. The fernery was where Victorian courting couples strolled, ostensibly admiring the flora.

5 WINTER GARDENS GLAS/CLYDE
Glasgow Green, Glasgow 0141 271 2962 *www.glasgowmuseums.com open Mon–Thurs and Sat, 10am–5pm, Fri and Sun 1pm–5pm*
Elegant and huge conservatory (1898) on Glasgow Green, enclosing the rear façade of the People's Palace. The Green has undergone a massive renovation, making it once again one of the great city parks. The Winter Gardens are supposedly designed to resemble the upturned hull of Nelson's flagship, HMS *Victory*. Enjoy Billy Connolly's enormous banana boots in the museum, then tea or coffee among the tropical plants.

29 QUIET BEACHES

1 CORAL BEACHES HIGHLANDS
Dunvegan, Skye *www.skyewalk.co.uk*
Drive past Dunvegan Castle car park, keep on going to the end of the road, park your car and walk along a farm track to the beach. It's an easy walk and the sand is lovely once you get there. It's not actually coral, apparently, but some kind of dried algae.

2 LONGNIDDRY BENTS EDIN/LOTH
Longniddry, East Lothian
A strand of gorgeous beaches in East Lothian, popular with sunseekers from Edinburgh but not nearly as busy at the sands further down the coast at Gullane. Children love pottering about in the rock pools and it's great for dogs. Don't be put off by the view of Cockenzie power station.

3 MANGERSTA OUT. ISLES
Lewis 01851 703 088 *(Lewis tourist information)*
On the far west coast of Lewis (follow B8011, then the even more minor road to Mangersta), this is a gem of a beach, incredibly secluded and probably one of the most unusual you will ever visit. You'll need to scrabble over dunes covered with a blanket of machair flowers and grasses and along a narrow strip of land to get there, but it's worth the effort. But while the beach is beautiful to look at, the seas are rough and too dangerous to swim in – so best not.

4 SANNA BAY HIGHLANDS
Ardnamurchan *(follow B8007 to just beyond Kilchoan, then take minor road to Sanna)*
Sanna Bay is the sort of beach people may be very surprised to find even exists in Scotland. Its fine white sands lapped by silvery blue water, make it well worth the arduous drive into the remotest wilds of west Scotland to get there. It has also inspired landscape artist John Lowrie Morrison; those lucky enough to have a chance to visit the beach will soon see why.

5 TANTALLON EDIN/LOTH
Near North Berwick, East Lothian
www.historic-scotland.gov.uk.
The beach out by Tantallon Castle costs a quid to get on, but it is out of the way (off the A198 east of North Berwick) and glorious.

6 TRAIGH EAIS OUT. ISLES
North-East Barra
Hidden over the dunes just 300 yards to the west of the spectacular Barra Airport, where planes take off from and land on the sand, lies another gem. Traigh Eais is a two-mile stretch of white sand and usually deserted. It's the perfect place to watch the Atlantic breakers crashing in on the Western Isles.

30 STYLE BARS

1 METROPOLITAN BAR GLAS/GLYDE
Candleriggs, Glasgow 0141 553 1488
www.metropolitan-bar.com
There are plenty of bars vying for attention in Glasgow's Merchant City, but this one stands out from the crowd – especially the after-work crowd. And once the suits have fled the city for the day, the Metropolitan is an ideal place to relax and be seen. Tucked beside the more casual Beer Café, this smart bar opens out on to an indoor courtyard at the back, giving the illusion of an outdoor drinking and dining experience all year round. The staff are quick and friendly – and there doesn't seem to be a drink they can't mix here.

2 VIBE BAR GLAS/CLYDE
ABode, 129 Bath St, Glasgow
0141 572 6014 *www.abodehotels.co.uk*
ABode has an excellent little basement bar. As part of Michael Caines' former Arthouse Hotel, you can rely on great food in a relaxed atmosphere.

3 TIGERLILY EDIN/LOTH
129 George Street, Edinburgh
0131 225 5005
www.tigerlilyedinburgh.co.uk
An obvious one. This place has been mentioned in Condé Naste's coolest hotels in the world list. Its bar is extremely hip with an amazing decor, but the drinks list is exhaustive and the

staff are friendly, which sets it apart from its various neighbours.

4 ÒRAN MÓR GLAS/CLYDE
Top of Byres Road, Glasgow
0141 357 6200 *www.oran-mor.co.uk*
The 2002 conversion of the old Kelvinside Parish Church at the top end of Byres Road into Òran Mór created a West End hotspot away from the studenty hubbub of Ashton Lane. The most underrated part of the venue, used for private functions and as an arts venue, is the bar area, which attracts a weekend crowd from across a broad spectrum of ages and tastes. You'd have to be an early bird to secure a table in this bar, but half the fun here is standing and circulating.

5 LINEN GLAS/CLYDE
1110 Pollokshaws Rd, Glasgow
0141 649 3815
Linen in Shawlands is a small but stylish bar, which always seems to have a real buzz about it. The house band (The Fortunate Sons) bring the place alive on Saturday nights and there's a real sense of camaraderie. Based in an old bank, it mixes opulent Victorian architecture with a sleek modern mezzanine and lighting.

31 GARDENS

1 LEITH HALL ABER/GRAMP
near Kennethmont, Huntly,
Aberdeenshire 0844 493 2175
www.nts.org.uk
The garden at Leith Hall is the National Trust for Scotland's hidden gem. Set well away from the house, it sits on the side of a south-facing hill. It deserves a lot more support in terms of numbers visiting. There are all sorts of features

worth seeing. The moon gate is outstanding and is a fairly uncommon feature in Scottish gardens. A moon gate is usually constructed from stone encircling the shape of the moon and you step through it at its lowest point which is at ground level. It is an excellent construction for framing a view or making an entrance to another part of a garden. The herbaceous and mixed borders are colourful from June into the autumn. The organic vegetable garden, protected from aphids and other beasties by French marigolds, is a joy to watch over a season. First-class produce is grown ensuring healthy eating for those fortunate enough to receive a share of the bounty.

2 ACHAMORE GARDENS WHLLS&T
Isle of Gigha 01583 505 275
www.gigha.org.uk
The large mature camelias are spectacular in April. There is also a large collection of rhododendrons and many other plants worth seeing. The proud peacocks put up a good display for visitors. The garden is owned by the Gigha Heritage Trust, which has been a great success for local people. The trust is in the process of raising £391,000 for the first phase of improvements to the gardens.

3 LOGAN BOTANIC GARDEN SOUTH SCOT
Port Logan, Galloway
01852 300 237 *www.rbge.org.uk*
This is a garden that is much loved by its public. It benefits from the Gulf Stream, which has become the North Atlantic Drift by the time it passes our shores. Many west coast gardens benefit from this warmer water, which provides warm moist air in the winds off the sea. There is no guarantee that

it will prevent winter frosts, however it does limit them and therefore limits frost damage to plants. Arum lilies flower really well out of doors on the edge of the pond, which is home to magnificent fish. Groves of *Dicksonia antartica*, the New Zealand tree fern, thrive outside. On the east coast in Edinburgh, the tree ferns have to be under glass at the Royal Botanic Garden. Take time to examine the cross-section of the tree fern trunk. You will see that the roots of this wonderful plant are on the outside of the trunk structure. Watering is achieved by wetting the trunk. Logan is part of the Royal Botanic Garden Edinburgh Trust.

4 THE GARDEN OF COSMIC SPECULATION SOUTH SCOT
Portrack House, Holywood, near Dumfries *www.charlesjencks.com*
A visit will turn all your ideas of garden design on their heads. This garden is unique. It is a landscape of curls, sweeps and spirals with expanses of water that create tranquillity. Your mind is challenged by what you see. The paradise garden is a good example of a traditional garden within the overall design. This is a private garden. It is open once a year as part of the Scotland's Gardens Scheme to raise money for Maggie's Cancer Caring Centres. Groups that would like to visit may apply in writing to Charles A Jencks, Portrack House, Holywood, Dumfries, DG2 0RW.

5 AN CALA *(The Haven)* WHLLS&T
Isle of Seil, near Oban 01852 300 237
Cross the bridge over the Atlantic south of Oban and you are on the way to visit a most interesting garden. The garden has an expansive feel about it, even

although it occupies a fairly small area. There is plenty to see including a fine *Lirodendron tulipifera*, the tulip tree, expansive borders of herbaceous plants, shrubs and small trees. The summer house is a must for children who can see cones and seeds organised in symmetrical designs. This is a private garden that opens under Scotland's Gardens Scheme. However, visitors are welcome at other times by arrangement.

6 LITTLE SPARTA EDIN/LOTH
Stonypath, Pentland Hills, Edinburgh
www.littlesparta.co.uk
Scotland's greatest work of outdoor art is surely Ian Hamilton Finlay's garden at Little Sparta, a fusion of sculpture, poetry and philosophical exploration that is equally striking in all weathers – although it is open only on Friday and Sunday afternoons, 2.30–5pm, from 15 June to 14 Oct. Visits by groups of 10 or more should be made by appointment: telephone Laura Robertson on 07758 812 263.

32 CRÊPES

1 LE SEPT EDIN/LOTH
5 Hunter Square, Edinburgh
0131 225 5428
If you don't give a second thought to the hardening of your arteries, then Le Sept is the ultimate venue for crêpes that are absolutely sodden with cheese and bechamel sauce. The crayfish and haddock one is the best, closely followed by the chicken and asparagus option, both of which come with a token bit of salad.

2 CRÊPE À CROISSANT GLAS/CLYDE
396 Byres Road, Glasgow 0141 339 7003
www.crepe.org.uk
There are four branches of this food

outlet in Glasgow (and one in Dubai), and it's a bit like Subway for Francophiles. Criticism aside, they've got a great selection of crêpes for vegetarians – try the curried chick pea version if you want to stay regular. For pudding, try a Cupid's Cup – a sweet crêpe packed with After Eights, flaked almonds, fresh cream and crème de menthe.

3 FRENCH CONNECTION EDIN/LOTH outside Usher Hall and in Grassmarket, Edinburgh

These vans, which have been a fixture on Edinburgh streets for years, make fast food more classy with their selection of savoury and sweet galettes. If you don't mind dripping Nutella all down your front, then that's the variety to go with. If you're in more of a savoury mood, the ham and cheese galette is good, too.

4 BROUGHTON DELICATESSEN

EDIN/LOTH 7 Barony Street, Edinburgh 0131 558 7111

This deli is great for takeaway cheese and cakes, but through the back is the pièce de résistance – a great little eatery, where you can have lovely crêpes with various meats and cheeses, all served on their signature bread boards. If you're popping by in the afternoon, try one of their pear and toffee galettes with an Americano.

5 BON APPETIT PAD&F
22–26 Exchange Street, Dundee 01382 809 000

Unpretentious and friendly little French restaurant which is great for a Dundonian pre-shopping carbohydrate fix, and the prices are reasonable enough for you to have deux, or even trois. Good choice of crêperie basics, the best of which is a smoked salmon, crème fraîche and chives version.

33 HIGH-LEVEL DRIVES

1 CAIRN O' MOUNT ABER/GRAMP
The B974 follows the line of an old military road connecting the quaint village of Fettercairn to Banchory in Strath Dee. It reaches its highest point at Cairn O' Mount, from where there are magnificent views over Lewis Grassic Gibbon's beloved Howe O' The Mearns.

2 SOUTRA SOUTH SCOT
The A68 south of Pathhead rises up via a series of sweeping bends before it plateaus out at Soutra. Here the driver can get up-close-and-personal with huge wind turbines. A short walk will take in the ruins of Soutra Aisle – the remains of a 12th-century Augustinian hospital and monastery.

3 WANLOCKHEAD SOUTH SCOT
The B797 connects the M74 with the A76 by means of a twisty, scarred valley that passes through the twin lead mining villages of Leadhills and Wanlockhead where Lanarkshire meets Dumfriesshire. At around 1,500ft above sea level, the latter settlement is Scotland's highest village and home to the fantastic lead mining museum.

4 COCKBRIDGE ABER/GRAMP
The A939 Corgarff to Tomintoul road is the most famous closed road in Britain. Connecting Strath Dee with Strath Spey, its biggest challenge for half the year seems to be finding it open. Just south of Cockbridge is the beautiful 16th-century Corgarff Castle.

5 BEALACH NA BA HIGHLANDS
(the pass of the cattle)

This unclassified old droving road between Kishorn and Applecross has the distinction of being the highest road in Scotland. It climbs through a series of precipitous hairpin bends to a height of 2,053 ft. But the slog to the top is rewarded with stunning views of Skye.

6 BRUAR TO KINLOCH RANNOCH
PAD&F

A beautiful drive through rural Highland Perthshire. Head from Bruar on the A9 to near Kinloch Rannoch by the B847, passing through Calvine, Struan and Trinafour.

7 INNERLEITHEN TO MIDDLETON
SOUTH SCOT – EDIN/LOTH

Go north from Innerleithen, near Peebles in the Scottish Borders, to near Middleton in Midlothian (A7) on the B7007.

8 OVER THE CAMPSIE FELLS PAD&F

Go west from Stirling to Kippen, then head south on to the B822 to Fintry before descending to Clachan of Campsie.

9 OVER THE LAMMERMUIRS
SOUTH SCOT

Drive from Duns (in the Borders) to Gifford on the B6355, then return via the unclassified road through Longformacus.

10 GILMERTON TO ABERFELDY
PAD&F

From Gilmerton, west of Perth (and slightly to the north-east of Crieff), go north (through Amulree) on the A822 to Cablea, then take the A826 to Aberfeldy as the A822 heads for Dunkeld.

34 OLD-FASHIONED PUBS

1 BENNET'S BAR EDIN/LOTH
8 Leven Street, Tollcross, Edinburgh
0131 229 5143

A fine example of a traditional Scottish pub with stained-glass windows, an intricate carved wooden gantry and traditional snug. Bennet's, which is next door to the King's Theatre, serves good food, a wide range of malt whiskies and has a tasty cask ale or two on tap. Its Green Room is popular with performers at the adjacent King's Theatre.

2 HORSESHOE BAR GLAS/CLYDE
17 Drury Lane *(off West Nile Street)*, Glasgow 0141 229 5711 *www.scotland. org.uk/food/horseshoe.htm*

The famous city-centre hostelry has the longest continuous bar in the UK, at 104 ft. Admire the Victorian decor while you sup one of their excellent ales. Those in search of tasty, cheap food can visit the upstairs lounge, where karaoke nights are also held and Pop Idol winner Michelle McManus once held sway.

3 THE GLOBE INN SOUTH SCOT
56 High Street, Dumfries 01387 252 335
www.globeinndumfries.co.uk

A favourite of Robert Burns, who even scratched a message to a lover in one of the upstairs rooms. The Globe was established in 1610, shortly after the Union of the Crowns, when James I and VI was on the throne. If you catch publican Jane Brown at a quiet moment and ask her nicely, she may tell you all about the pub's rich past.

4 PRINCE OF WALES ABER/GRAMP
7 St Nicholas Lane, Aberdeen
01224 640 597
Thought to have the longest straight
bar in Scotland, at about 60 ft, it is
noted for its traditional interior and is
one of the Granite City's best pubs.
Known for its real ale and eclectic mix
of clientele – students, city workers and
those in search of a homely refuge from
style bars. A favourite with local and
visiting climbers.

5 STEIN INN HIGHLANDS
Waternish, Skye 01470 592 362
www.stein-inn.co.uk
The oldest inn on Skye, the Stein dates
back to 1790, although parts of the
building are older. On the shores of a
sea loch, it boasts outstanding views
that guests and drinkers can enjoy
while sipping one of about 100
whiskies. This selection has seen the inn
recognised as a 'Whisky Embassy' by the
Scotch Whisky Tourism Initiative. It also
has its own cask ale, Reeling Deck.

35 SPOTS FOR STARGAZING

1 MILLS OBSERVATORY PAD&F
Balgay Park, Dundee 01382 435967
www.dundeecity.gov.uk/mills
As the only full-time public observatory
in the UK, the Mills is an excellent place
for those who want to learn more
about astronomy and the sky at night.
The trees on Balgay Hill shield the
observatory from the city centre's
sodium street lights. Under its papier-
mâché dome, the observatory houses a
10in refractor, ideal for watching the
planets and offering great views of the
moon. The large viewing deck on the
roof offers an open view of the night
sky and, in the daytime, an excellent
view down to the Firth of Tay.

2 ROYAL OBSERVATORY EDIN/LOTH
Blackford Hill, Edinburgh 0131 668 8100
www.roe.ac.uk/vc
Atop Blackford Hill, the Royal
Observatory has an excellent visitor
centre and offers regular talks and
observing evenings during the winter
months. During the daytime, the view
from the roof offers a unique vista of
the Edinburgh skyline but at night the
deck really comes into its own, giving
visitors the chance to see planets and
stars, with help on hand from the
experts if need be. The site is still an
active science centre, with new
instruments being made for the next
generation of telescopes.

3 WEST SANDS PAD&F
St Andrews, Fife *www.fife.gov.uk*
It may be more famous as the location
for the beach scene from *Chariots of
Fire*, but West Sands in St Andrews is
also a pretty good spot for a wee bit of
stargazing. On a clear night, when the
clouds aren't rolling in, the sand dunes
behind it are great for setting up a
telescope. If the atmosphere and the
sun conspire, then the beach can also
be an excellent spot for watching the
aurora borealis.

4 CAWDOR WOOD HIGHLANDS
Cawdor, Nairn, Moray
www.cawdorcastle.com
Forests may seem like an odd choice
when it comes to astronomy, but
clearings can be a great place to
stargaze. For starters, try the 'Big
Wood' at Cawdor, near Nairn.

5 ROTHIEMURCHUS ESTATE

HIGHLANDS **Aviemore, Inverness-shire**
www.rothiemurchus.net
There are so many great locations in
the Spey Valley that it's hard to single
out one – but some of the spots inside
Rothiemurchus Estate, near Aviemore,
are truly superb.

36 BREAKFASTS

1 SNAX EDIN/LOTH
118 Buccleuch Street, Edinburgh
0131 557 8688
This has a brilliant atmosphere in which
to enjoy your all-day breakfast. Opera
music sets the tone and staff make all
welcome, not just regulars. A
traditional all-day breakfast with
sausage, beans, fried egg, black
pudding and toast starts at £2.30. The
bigger version is £3.70, while the
spectacular version is £3.80. Snax is also
at 15 West Register Street, 45–46
London Road, Edinburgh.

2 LEFT BANK GLAS/CLYDE
33–35 Gibson Street, Glasgow
0141 339 5969
From an Ayrshire bacon ciabatta to a
Bombay breakfast (dhal, Bombay
potatoes, yoghurt and warmed flat
bread), this place adds an authentic,
original twist to the most important
meal of the day. The eggs mornay,
which come with spinach and smoked
salmon, are especially delicious.

3 PECKHAM'S GLAS/CLYDE
61–65 Glassford St, Glasgow
0141 553 0666 *www.peckhams.co.uk*
This deli chain has long been the home
of the best caramel shortcake in the
world, and a great off-licence and late-
night rendezvous point. It comes as no

surprise breakfast and brunch are such
a treat. Wake up with tea or fresh juice
and tuck into eggs, French toast, Italian
biscuits or selection of cheeses. Also at
Byres Road, Clarence Drive and
Hyndland Road, Glasgow, plus Prestwick
Airport, Lenzie and Newton Mearns
plus Bruntsfield Place, Raeburn Place
and South Clerk Street, Edinburgh (see
website for details).

4 HADRIAN'S BRASSERIE EDIN/LOTH
Balmoral Hotel, Edinburgh
0131 557 5000
More and more people rejoice in the
fact that it's possible to breakfast on the
hoof, grabbing a bagel, a granola
smoothie – even a pot of takeaway
porridge. But there is still something to
be said for the elegant, starched-linen
breakfast at table. Few places do it
better than Hadrian's. On a bright
morning, it can be flooded with sunlight
and is great for celeb-spotting. There's a
groaning breakfast buffet table, plus the
usual mixed grill and eggs on a hotplate
under silver salvers. For the time-poor,
order from the menu – its smoked
salmon and scrambled is near-perfect.

5 URBAN ANGEL EDIN/LOTH
121 Hanover St, Edinburgh
0131 225 6215
If you can get in at the weekend, go to
Urban Angel. Their eggs Benedict is the
ideal way to see off a hangover and
with everything produced in as fairly
traded a way as possible, it makes this
calorie-laden dish as guilt-free as it
can be.

37 CHOCOLATIERS

1 MAYA HIGHLANDS
Strathpeffer, Ross-shire 01997 420 008

www.mayachocolates.co.uk
Master Chocolatier Fabienne De Mulder
hails from Belgium and brings chocolate
excellence to Scotland. Fabienne works
in a studio that looks on to the coffee
shop so customers can watch Fabienne
create delicacies like butter cream
truffles and Earl Grey tea chocolates.

2 BELGIAN CALEDONIAN
CHOCOLATE LINE HIGHLANDS
**Victorian Market, Inverness, and High
Street, Fortrose 01381 622 302**
Lucas and Ingrid Storey's handmade
Belgian chocolates are truly something
special. Located in Inverness's Victorian
Market, this chocolate heaven sits
beside shops selling Scottish souvenirs,
needlework and heraldic art and
design.

3 COCOA MOUNTAIN HIGHLANDS
Durness, Sutherland 01971 511 233
www.cocoamountain.co.uk
Cocoa Mountain chocolates are lovingly
made by hand, using only the finest
ingredients, without any additional
preservatives. James Findlay and Paul
Maiden first set up shop in June 2006
after varied careers. Now they live in
the tranquillity of Durness and are
possibly the most remote chocolate
producers in Europe.

4 ANANDA CHOCOLATES EDIN/LOTH
07795 420 001
www.thinkingchocolate.com
A fast-growing newcomer on the block,
producing to-die-for hand-made
chocolates in Edinburgh (the name
'Ananda' comes from anandamide,
reportedly the chemical found in
chocolate that makes you feel good).
Chilli and orange truffles, strawberry
and rose chocs and boxes made of

chocolate are specialities; for Valentine's
Day, they make solid chocolate hearts in
gold leaf. Outlets include the Manna
House on Easter Road and The Store in
Stockbridge, or order direct.

5 HOT CHOCOLATES EDIN/LOTH
**255 St John's Road, Corstorphine,
Edinburgh 0131 477 9902**
www.hotchocolates.biz
Absolutely delicious – try eating just
one – hand-tempered chocolate and
hand-dipped centres. Sharon and Chris
won the Guild of Fine Food's 'Best New
Product of the Show' award for their
apple crumble chocolate. Especially
recommended is the 'El Gordo'
selection.

38 TRAIN JOURNEYS

1 GLASGOW – MALLAIG GLAS/CLYDE
– HIGHLANDS
The glorious West Highland line is a
five-hour treat providing spectacular
views of the industrial Firth of Clyde,
bleak Rannoch Moor, and the inner
Hebrides over the final stretch. First
ScotRail's diesel multiple units may not
do justice to the scenery, but they are
being refurbished, and the Jacobite
steam train plies the Fort William –
Mallaig section.

2 DUNDEE – EDINBURGH PAD&F –
EDIN/LOTH
A trip that takes in two of Scotland's
greatest railway bridges, over the Tay
and the Forth, along with fabulous
views of Dundee and the Queensferry
passage respectively. A sense of
anticipation grows as the train hugs the
Fife coastline directly opposite
Edinburgh as it heads southwards,
before a series of tunnels brings you

out on to the Victorian engineering marvel.

3 PERTH – INVERNESS PAD&F – HIGHLANDS

Best appreciated on waking from slumber aboard the London sleeper as it makes the final leg of its 570 mile journey to the Highland capital. Dramatic sights include the gorge of the River Garry at Killiecrankie and ascending to the 1,484 ft Drumochter summit near Dalwhinnie, the highest point on the British rail network.

4 EDINBURGH – NEWCASTLE
EDIN/LOTH – SOUTH SCOT

The train looks as if it may topple over the cliffs on this spectacular coastal section of the east coast main line, which also takes in the glorious sweep of the 28-arch Royal Border Bridge at Berwick-upon-Tweed. The views look even better over lunch in a dining car.

5 AYR – STRANRAER SOUTH SCOT

A Cinderella line that may appear to follow a circuitous route to the gateway to Northern Ireland, but can provide a faster and less stressful alternative to the twisty A77, temporarily ensconcing the passenger in the tranquil rural wastes of south-west Scotland.

More info: www.steamtrain.info

39 ROMANTIC RESTAURANTS

1 DOMENICO'S EDIN/LOTH
30 Sandport Street, Leith, Edinburgh
0131 467 7266

With only a handful of tables, this off the beaten track Italian gem feels like something you'd dream of stumbling upon in Rome or Florence. The food is authentic, the portions huge, the wine reasonably priced and the service always friendly and infallible. And if the truffle bruschetta or antipasti platter doesn't get your heart racing, nothing will.

2 MARRIOTT DALMAHOY HOTEL
EDIN/LOTH Kirknewton, near Edinburgh
0131 333 1845 www.marriott.co.uk

The Dalmahoy is certainly up there with the best places in Edinburgh for fine dining if not the best place in the capital – the food is exquisite. Slightly off the beaten track, it is far enough away from the hustle and bustle of the city centre and the surroundings are peaceful and of course romantic – a great venue to propose. It's worth going that bit out of town for something different, to enjoy the food of love.

3 CAFÉ ST HONORE EDIN/LOTH
34 Thistle Street Lane North West, Edinburgh 0131 226 2211

With its French waiters and mirror-panelled walls, you could almost believe you're in Paris. Food is French-style with fresh Scottish ingredients – simple but great, and certainly very romantic.

4 INVER COTTAGE RESTAURANT
WHLLS&T Strathlachlan, Argyll
01369 860 537 www.invercottage.co.uk

Small, intimate place with amazing views and incredible food. Starting life as a croft and ferryman's home, it overlooks Old Castle Lachlan, sacked by the Campbells after Culloden. Now a listed ruin, the old castle provides a splendid backdrop to the setting sun. The restaurant has kept the tradition of ancient Scottish hospitality with two huge blazing log fires in the winter and scrubbed oak tables. Service is attentive, without being fussy or formal, and the place has a very intimate atmosphere. Local fish and meats are a speciality – scallops are hand-picked by divers, salmon is from the Kyles of Bute, langoustine and halibut are brought by boat daily, venison stalked in the area. A restaurant which just has everything right: location, food and atmosphere. If that doesn't put you in a romantic mood, nothing will.

5 THE GRILL ROOM EDIN/LOTH
1 Festival Square, The Sheraton Hotel, Edinburgh 0131 229 9131
www.starwoodhotels.com/sheraton
Intimate surroundings and discreet staff who love to indulge romantic diners. It also demonstrates to a loved one that you're prepared to splash out on them. For meat lovers, there's the additional bliss of Australian prime Wagyu beef, hand-massaged for tenderness, fed on a diet of beer and grain to ensure extraordinary taste and marbling, while listening to Mozart. The cow is basically sent into a rapture of ecstasies within its lifetime, to ensure an equivalent result on the diner's taste buds.

6 KILBERRY INN WHLLS&T
Kilberry, Argyll 01880 770 223
www.kilberryinn.com
A rustic and romantic inn on one of the UK's most traffic-free roads – with awesome food.

7 VINTNERS ROOMS EDIN/LOTH
87 Giles Street, Leith 0131 554 6767
www.thevintnersrooms.com
Forget the flowers and the chocolates, the serenades and the glittering jewels and instead save up your hard-earned cash for a night of pure pleasure at this fine Leith restaurant. The candlelit vaulted dining rooms, the smooth tones of your host, Silvio, and a menu laced with the divine trinity of foie gras, caviar and truffles conspire to make this the perfect spot for wining and dining your beloved.

8 THE ORANGERY PAD&F
Balbirnie House, Markinch, Fife
01592 610 066 *www.balbirnie.co.uk*
Set the romantic mood by sweeping up the drive of the 416-acre estate to be met by the imposing front columns of a Georgian mansion. The Orangery has been renovated in art-deco style and offers modern European fare with a seafood emphasis. Service is friendly and discreet. Be sure to take coffee in the cosy lounge afterwards, where hopefully you will get cosier still.

9 THE CRICKLEWOOD HOTEL
GLAS/CLYDE **27 Hamilton Rd, Bothwell**
01698 853 172
Whether you are planning on whispering sweet nothings or enjoying sweet treats, avoid the modern city centre restaurants and head for a romantic meal in a traditional setting. A trip to The Cricklewood is a weekend mini-break in a single evening. This whitewashed hotel has a country pub feel and a distinctive Scottish flavour to its menu. But the real secret to its success is the absence of open planning. The nooks and crannies mean that, even when the restaurant is full, you can enjoy privacy for a intimate tête-à-tête over your meal.

10 ARDANAISEIG HOTEL PAD&F
Kilchrenan by Taynuilt 01866 833 333
www.ardanaiseig.com
Overlooking the lawns which run down

to the banks of Loch Tay, the dining room has the perfect backdrop to invite romance. The menu – sporting the freshest Scottish ingredients – is fantastic and the tables are thoughtfully well-spaced, making it easier to partake in couple talk. There's also a log fire in the library next to which you can enjoy a cosy nightcap.

40 HIDDEN SHOPPING GEMS

1 ASIMI JEWELLERY EDIN/LOTH
**40 George Street, Edinburgh
0131 220 5070 *www.asimi.co.uk***
Asimi is full of really stunning jewellery. The owner, Sheila Dafereras, sources all the products from Greece so you're guaranteed to find something really different and unusual. Prices range from around £5 to hundreds of pounds, which is great, as you can always pick up something – whether a 'wee minding' or a special gift.

2 PAPYRUS GLAS/CLYDE
**220 Buchanan Galleries, Glasgow
0141 331 1437 *www.papyrusgifts.co.uk***
This is a really fun shop – they have everything from funny, novelty gifts to cool and funky stuff for the home. Particular favourites are the retro products like the Hello Kitty range and old Beatles bags, and the Scottish gifts they sell like tartan piggy banks and dialect mugs. Papyrus is also home to a really wide range of Hot Diamonds jewellery which make excellent presents.

3 MUTTS NUTS EDIN/LOTH
**50 High Street, Edinburgh
0131 225 7710**

One for those who like something a bit wacky! The shop has a bit of a cult following and is jam-packed with really quirky trinkets and toys. It's a real find for music lovers as they have tons of products inspired by legendary bands like The Who, the Beatles and the Sex Pistols. The walls of the store are covered in steel signs from cool brands like Jack Daniel's, Lambretta, Vespa and my favourite – Betty Boop.

4 ART LOVERS' SHOP GLAS/CLYDE
House for an Art Lover, Bellahouston Park, Glasgow 0141 353 4770
This one is a real hidden gem, as part of the gorgeous House for an Art Lover in Glasgow's Bellahouston Park. It is full of unique, stylish items including beautiful cards, stationery, home-wear items and jewellery by local designers. One of the girls who works in the shop, Vanessa Livesley, is a jewellery designer and sells her lovely pieces there. The store is so elegant, and in such a beautiful location, that it's a lovely place to visit.

5 ILLUMINATI GLAS/CLYDE
Princes Square, Glasgow 0141 221 8787
I especially love Illuminati for the gorgeous choice of intricate cards they stock – many of them are handmade and they really add a special touch to a gift. The shop is full of really pretty, girly things like vintage-style tea sets, cute compacts and sparkly things, so it's great for picking up gifts. It is also a great place to find unusual wedding gifts as they stock a selection of unique 'bride and groom' presents.

41 ISLAND TOWNS

1 TOBERMORY WHLLS&T
Mull *www.tobermory.co.uk*

Made famous by the children's television programme *Balamory*, the main street of Tobermory is an attractive and colourful array of houses, shops and tourist accommodation. It is Mull's main town, at the north end of the island, and is a hive of activity in summer. The view across the harbour from the poignant war memorial on the hill behind the town is particularly stunning.

2 PORTREE HIGHLANDS
Skye
www.visithighlands.com/skye/portree
Like that of Tobermory, the main street of Skye's biggest town curls around the harbour. The houses of Portree harbour are less bright than those of Tobermory, but are painted in gentle and attractive pale pinks and blues. Portree's position on the island makes it an excellent base from which to explore Skye, from the Trotternish Peninsula in the north to the Black Cuillin in the south.

3 KIRKWALL OUT. ISLES
Orkney *www.visitorkney.com*
Once at the heart of a seafaring empire stretching from Scandinavia to Iceland, the main town in northerly Orkney has a culture distinct from the Scottish mainland and the islands of the west. Kirkwall is in many ways a Scandinavian town rather than a Scottish one and really was one until it was acquired by James III of Scotland in 1468. It is now the bustling hub of life in modern Orkney.

4 STORNOWAY OUT. ISLES
Lewis *www.visithebrides.com*
Stornoway is the largest town in the Western Isles and its ferry service links Lewis to the mainland at Ullapool. Its busy harbour is home to a sizeable fishing fleet and much tourist traffic.

As Sabbath observance remains a feature of life on Lewis and Harris, shops, many pubs, businesses and restaurants in Stornoway continue to close on Sundays and few transport links operate.

5 LOCHMADDY OUT. ISLES
North Uist *www.visithebrides.com*
Lochmaddy lies at the north end of the chain of Outer Hebridean islands that includes Berneray, North Uist, Benbecula, South Uist and Barra. Ferries link the biggest town on North Uist with Uig on Skye. Lochmaddy is another attractive village with a beautiful harbour setting and is a great location to see some magnificent west coast sunsets.

42 PLACES TO SEE SALMON LEAPING

1 FALLS OF BRAAN PAD&F
The Hermitage, Dunkeld, Perthshire
0844 493 2192 *www.nts.org.uk*
The Falls of Braan and the associated romantic folly of Ossian's Hall were an integral part of Perthshire romantic tours during the 18th century. Today, the Braan Walk follows a waymarked riverside and woodland path for six kms and is certainly one of the most picturesque locations to watch salmon leaping.

2 FALLS OF SHIN HIGHLANDS
Achany Glen, Lairg, Sutherland
01549 402 231 *www.fallsofshin.co.uk*
The River Shin flows into one of the great salmon rivers of the Highlands, the River Oykel. Situated midway between Bonar Bridge and Lairg in Achany Glen is the Falls of Shin Visitor

Centre. From the visitor centre, a series of woodland walks loop to viewing points over the spectacular waterfalls. The visitor centre has a gift shop and restaurant, and sells Harrods' goods.

3 PHILIPHAUGH SALMON VIEWING CENTRE SOUTH SCOT **near Selkirk, Scottish Borders 01896 849 723** *www.salmonviewingcentre.com*
The Salmon Viewing Centre on the Philiphaugh Estate, near Selkirk, is a remarkable visitor attraction. Members of the public can witness the epic migration of the salmon in their natural habitat – both above and below the water's surface – thanks to live video links from underwater cameras sited in the Ettrick Water.

4 PITLOCHRY DAM AND SALMON LADDER PAD&F **Perthshire 01796 473 152** *www.scottish-southern.co.uk*
Pitlochry is synonymous with the salmon's incredible journey due to the famous hydro-electric dam and salmon ladder that receives an estimated half a million visitors each year. The salmon ladder is more than 300 m in length and consists of 34 chambers, which allow more than 5,000 fish to progress upstream to Loch Faskally and beyond.

5 GLEN TANAR ESTATE ABER/GRAMP **Deeside 01339 886 072** *www.glentanar.co.uk*
The Braeloine Visitor Centre on the Glen Tanar Estate is fully equipped with visitor facilities, car parking and a full-time ranger service. The rangers can provide specific advice on the best spots to watch salmon on one of Scotland's most famous rivers. Timing is crucial – the fish tend to be more active in the

early morning and evening, especially after a spell of heavy rain (when the river levels tend to rise).

43 BOATING PONDS

1 CRAIGTOUN COUNTRY PARK PAD&F **By St Andrews 01334 473 666** *www.visit-standrews.co.uk/ craigtouncountrypark.cfm*
Originally forming part of the grounds of Mount Melville House, Craigtoun was established as a country park in 1947. The fabulous boating pond has swans and a full-size mock chateau on one side that you can sail into. The park also has aviaries, crazy golf, adventure playgrounds and a miniature railway that runs round the lake. Open April–Sept, 10.30am–6.30pm, last admission 5.30pm

2 STATION PARK SOUTH SCOT **Moffat** *www.visitmoffat.co.uk*
This has to be one of the best small-town parks in Scotland and must be archetypal of what most Scottish towns had in their Victorian and Edwardian heydays. There is a floral-arch entrance and the lovely, compact boating pond is surrounded by mature trees, beautiful flower beds and neatly-trimmed lawns. Guaranteed to bring back childhood memories for anyone over 40.

3 CAMPERDOWN PARK PAD&F **Coupar Angus Road, Dundee 01382 431 818** *www.camperdownpark.com*
Named after the famous naval battle off the Dutch coast in 1797, when Admiral Adam Duncan defeated the might of the Dutch navy. His pension from this built a large neo-classical mansion, which lies at the heart of this

extensive park. Fitting then that it should have a boating pond. The pond is actually a small reservoir known as Clatto Reservoir, which also hosts fishing.

4 AGNEW PARK SOUTH SCOT
Agnew Crescent, Stranraer
01776 703 535 *www.dumgal.gov.uk*
Situated close to the waterfront, this park draws heavily on Stranraer's maritime heritage as the main sailing point between Scotland and Ireland. There is a large boating pond with a variety of craft from which to choose. A play island has been created in the pond and connected to the shore by a small bridge. There is also the ubiquitous miniature railway, crazy golf, etc.

5 CALLENDAR PARK WHLLS&T
Falkirk 01324 506 070 *(Falkirk Council)*
Described by the local council as the jewel in its collection of parks, Callendar Park consists of 170 acres surrounding the fine and historic baronial mansion of Callendar House. The boating pond has characteristic swan pedalos for hire. The park itself has a profusion of flowers and woodlands to enjoy and hosts various events, including concerts.

44 CITY VIEWPOINTS

1 DUNDEE LAW PAD&F
Is there any city in Britain with a better view of itself than can be obtained from Dundee Law? It's a short uphill walk from the centre to this 571 ft volcanic plug, which gives an amazing 360 degree view over the city, bounded by the Sidlaw Hills to the north and stretching way over the Tay estuary to the kingdom of Fife. You can overlook

the Tay bridges, old jute mills, the rejuvenated city centre and the riverside with RRS *Discovery* as its centrepiece. Truly, in the words of McGonagall, the view is 'a sight most magnificent to be seen'.

2 TORRY BATTERY ABER/GRAMP
Aberdeen
Built in 1860 to guard against sea-borne attack, the battery gives electrifying views over harbour, city and coast. Great place to watch the boats. About 45 vessels a day enter and leave the busy port, including colourful, and sometimes strange, oilrig supply and support vessels, Shetland ferries, tankers and freighters. Dolphins can be spotted leaping in the harbour entrance.

3 CALTON HILL EDIN/LOTH
(off Waterloo Place) **Edinburgh**
Around the melange of monuments on the 355 ft lump of rock, an outlier of the Arthur's Seat volcano, the outlook is sweeping. View the length of Princes Street by day or night. Follow the roads, roofs, crescents and terraces, parks and gardens of Edinburgh down to a vast panorama across the Firth of Forth to the coastal towns and hills of Fife.

4 KESSOCK BRIDGE HIGHLANDS
Inverness
The Kessock Bridge carries the A9 north of Inverness, replacing a ferry in 1982. Walk along the River Ness from the city centre and out across the bridge. Hang on to your hats for the breathtaking view: to the right, the Moray Firth; to the left, the river-threaded and hillbound city, and up to the end of the Beauly Firth, with the 343 ft Ben Wyvis poking up in the distance.

5 GLASGOW NECROPOLIS
GLAS/CLYDE

At the highest point of Glasgow's City of the Dead, John Knox stands on his column. And if his stony eyes could see, I hope he would take pleasure in the prospect – a vista of the city and the Clyde valley stretching away to the hills and moors of south Lanarkshire and across to the Pentlands. Tinto Hill, 30 miles away, is visible on a clear day.

45 CHEESE SHOPS

1 I J MELLIS *stores in Edinburgh*
EDIN/LOTH *Glasgow* GLAS/CLYDE *and St Andrews* PAD&F **0131 661 9955**
www.ijmellischeesemonger.com
There is really only one great cheese shop in Scotland – Ian Mellis, with shops in Victoria Street and Stockbridge, Edinburgh, and Great Western Road, Glasgow, among others. Great collection of proper, individual farm-made cheeses. The smell hits you yards down the street and the staff let you try before you buy.

2 MITCHELLS SOUTH SCOT
**40–44 Bridge Street, Kelso
01573 450 272**
Mitchells has recently been taken over by George Lees, a butcher with a great reputation for local produce, but it hasn't altered the great array of cheeses from across the globe. A genuine Aladdin's cave of wild and wonderful produce that attracts tourists and locals in equal measure.

3 ARRAN ISLAND CHEESE COMPANY SOUTH SCOT
**Home Farm, Brodick, Arran
01770 302 788** *www.islandcheese.co.uk*
You can watch the cheesemakers in action at the shop, next to its dairy.

Sample the delicious cheeses and buy them from the wee shop. You can also buy the cheese from their shop in Ayr or from many farmers' markets.

4 DUNDEE CONTINENTAL MARKET
PAD&F **High Street, Dundee**
www.dundeecity.gov.uk
I love buying pick-and-mix bags of cheeses from here. You normally get a bag of four for about a fiver. They are usually held in July (with farmers' markets every month) – but a word of warning: if you do opt for the cheeses, make sure you've got a good tub to keep them in, otherwise they'll stink out the fridge.

5 THE PORK, CHEESE AND PIE SHOP HIGHLANDS
36 Eastgate, Inverness 01463 237 776
www.tasteofmoray.co.uk
It sounds like the perfect name for a shop – and the food's not bad either. The pies are delicious but it's the cheese that really shines.

46 VICTORIAN SPA TOWNS

1 STRATHPEFFER HIGHLANDS
The best example of a purpose-built Victorian spa town in Scotland, and the most northerly. Its transformation from a sleepy backwater followed the publication of work by Dr Morrison of Aberdeenshire, who extolled the curative powers of its sulphurous spring. With the support of the sympathetic Countess of Cromarty, a new resort was established. The variety of architecture on display is fantastic. There remains a pump house where at times the waters can still be sampled.

2 MOFFAT SOUTH SCOT

Long recognised for the healing powers of its mineral wells that led to the building of a Bath Hall in 1827. This was followed in 1878 by the opening of the 'palatial' Moffat Hydropathic Hotel, with more than 300 rooms. Sadly, this was destroyed by fire in 1921. Moffat remains a beautiful town in a beautiful location in a bowl of hills, which continues to make it a popular destination with holidaymakers and day-trippers alike.

3 BRIDGE OF ALLAN WHLLS&T

It's hard to think of it now, but Bridge of Allan as we know it today owes its origins to the Victorian obsession with spas. It became the haunt of wealthy Victorian families from Glasgow and Edinburgh who built or bought holiday property in the then village and came to 'take the waters'.

4 INNERLEITHEN SOUTH SCOT

Although usually thought of as a mill town, Innerleithen (alongside neighbouring Peebles) was also a long-established spa on the back of the reputation of the Dow well. Visited by Burns in 1787, it was described by him as famous. Its spa status rose with Sir Walter Scott's novel *St Ronan's Well*. The name stuck and a pump house and verandah were built. Still has a sampling pavilion.

5 BALLATER ABER/GRAMP

Quintessential Royal Deeside village initially established as a spa in the late 18th century. It was the arrival of Queen Victoria at nearby Balmoral and the subsequent establishment of a rail-head at Ballater that finally cemented the town's reputation for the masses. It really was the place to be seen in and it hosted a whole line of famous visitors including the Tsar of Russia. Among its architectural gems there is a Telford bridge.

47 FISHING FOR BEGINNERS

1 THE TAY PAD&F

01573 470 612 *www.fishtay.co.uk*
Arguably Scotland's greatest salmon river, the Tay flows from the loch at Kenmore through spectacular countryside to the sea at Perth. Salmon fishing can be expensive, but this is not always the case, and a day's fishing can be had in spring relatively cheaply. Trout are abundant and can reach up to 5 lb, but almost the entire catchment area is under a protection order, so permission is needed from the appropriate club, who will supply a permit for a modest fee. See the website for more details.

2 THE TWEED SOUTH SCOT

www.fishtweed.co.uk or
www.tweedguide.com
The Tweed produces large numbers of salmon every year and is a wonderful trout river. Beginners who just want to try it out can buy a package trip to and from Edinburgh. Three hours of tuition for two adults and two children, for instance, costs at least £150, but check out what's on offer and how much it costs at the website.

3 LAKE OF MENTEITH WHLLS&T

01877 385 664 *www.menteith-fisheries.co.uk*
Regarded by many as Scotland's premier competition venue and home to a wide

range of birdlife as well as rainbow and brown trout. There are 30 boats and an angling station providing tea and coffee. Stocked with 1,200 fish a week, so your chances are more than fair.

4 INVERAWE FISHERIES SOUTH SCOT
Argyll 01866 822 777
Another fishery providing sport for all abilities. There is salmon fishing on the River Awe and rainbow fishing in three lochs stocked daily. Hugo's Loch, with its smaller trout, is ideal for beginners.

48 SWEET SHOPS

1 GORDON AND DURWARD PAD&F
14 West High Street, Crieff, Perthshire
01764 653 800
Quaint, old-style sweet shop in Crieff and home of the 'famous sugar mice'. Enough mixed boilings to melt the nation's teeth and a sweet factory in the back where you can gawp for hours at them handmaking their sugary offerings. It trumps other sweet shops hands down for the quality of their produce, particularly mouth-watering macaroons, finger-licking fudge and quite possibly the best tablet in Scotland.

2 MOFFAT TOFFEE SHOP SOUTH
SCOT **High Street, Moffat**
01683 220 032
Returning home to Scotland up the M6 wouldn't be complete without a stop in Moffat to sample the delights of the toffee shop. It has about 200 different jars running along the shop shelves, alongside the famous toffee, made for more than 100 years. Flavours on offer include heather honey, ginger and chocolate, as well as their delicious vanilla tablet.

3 JOHNSONS FUDGE SHOP
WHLLS&T **Main Street, Callander**
01877 330 117
Whether you're heading up to the Highlands or threading your way through to the west coast, Callander is an excellent stopping-off point to stretch your legs. What better way to break a long car journey than popping in to sample some of the local fudge?

4 THE TODDLE IN EDIN/LOTH
7 Cockburn Street, Edinburgh
0131 225 1021
The ideal place for a child to spend their pocket money or for a nostalgic trip to revisit their favourite childhood sweets. There are rows of glass jars brimming with the likes of soor plooms, toffee doddles, pineapple chunks, rosy apples, rhubarb and custards, bon-bons and liquorice, to name but a few. Prices start at 82p for 100g, rising to over £1 for more expensive treats. This family-run business has a wonderful atmosphere.

5 JIM GARRAHY'S FUDGE KITCHEN
EDIN/LOTH **30 High Street, Edinburgh**
0131 558 1517
www.fudge-kitchen.co.uk
A bit of a tourist trap on the Royal Mile but worth nipping in to sample the delicious plates of fudge on the counter. You can grab a piece and run, but you're likely to run back and buy a big slab or two. You can also watch the fudge being made.

49 SEAFOOD RESTAURANTS

1 FISHERS IN THE CITY EDIN/LOTH
58 Thistle St, Edinburgh 0131 225 5109
www.fishersbistros.co.uk

Yes, there is a branch of Fishers on the atmospheric Shore, but this is a really good city-centre choice for fish fans. The menu invariably offers interesting as well as traditional choices and also has a good wine list. Nice atmosphere if you don't mind seeing gangs of City blokes hammering expense accounts.

2 THE SEAFOOD RESTAURANT
PAD&F 16 West End, St Monans, Fife
01333 730 327
www.theseafoodrestaurant.com
This former 'scampi in a basket' eatery has been brought up to award-winning standard over a decade by East Neuk seafood heroes Tim Butler and Craig Smith. Ask for a window seat to enjoy the views of the Forth and tuck into wonderful seafood in the knowledge you're getting equally excellent produce at better prices than American golfers are paying at its plusher sister restaurant in St Andrews.

3 CELLAR RESTAURANT PAD&F
24 East Green, Anstruther, Fife
01333 310 378
For a special meal out, the Cellar, with its cobbled courtyard, is tucked away behind the Scottish Fisheries Museum. Proprietor Peter Jukes was Scottish Restaurant Chef of the Year 2002; his atmospheric establishment serves freshly caught fare, such as signature crayfish bisque gratin, delicious scallops and fillet of roast cod with a pesto crust. Not cheap, reflecting three AA rosettes, but a real experience and set lunch is good value.

4 SWEET MELINDA'S EDIN/LOTH
11 Roseneath Street, Edinburgh
0131 229 7953
A seafood restaurant removed from the bustle of the city centre – which makes it feel like a real find – but convenient enough to be an accessible, busy and loved dining hot-spot. The chefs offer a variety of well-priced, tasty and beautifully presented dishes, complemented by a wine list to suit the palate and budget of most seafood lovers. The owners are certain enough in their cuisine to offer a weekly 'pay what you think it's worth' evening; put this to the test and confirm their fishy brilliance.

5 EAST HAUGH HOUSE HOTEL PAD&F
Pitlochry 01796 473 121
www.easthaugh.co.uk
This is a great place, with incredible, delicious dishes, such as scallops wrapped in bacon.

50 PLACES FOR TEENAGERS TO EAT

1 TGI FRIDAYS EDIN/LOTH
26 Castle Street, Edinburgh
0131 226 6543
The portions of food in the remodelled TGI Edinburgh are ridiculously large. This means when you've finished your meal, not only have you had a very enjoyable burger, steak or fajita, but you also feel proud. You're proud when your mates can't finish the 'share size' portions they got to themselves. The huge posters of Hendrix and Marley watching you eat are a bonus. The non-alcoholic smoothies are truly gorgeous but after the food you will probably need a taxi home.

2 GIULIANOS EDIN/LOTH
18–19 Union Street, Edinburgh
0131 556 6590

Classic Italian food, every type of pizza you would want and a big selection of pasta. Staff are very polite and enjoy having friendly banter with customers. They seem to be big football fans and you can have great fun discussing Italian football with them: the street outside was an absolute party after Italy won the World Cup in 2006. The puddings are quite special as well.

3 LA FAVORITA EDIN/LOTH
325 Leith Walk, Edinburgh
0131 554 2430
Cooked in wood-fired ovens, the pizza here is exceptionally good. Again, they do also have a range of pasta but the pizza is definitely the highlight. The huge glass windows at the front mean you can glance out at the Leithers going up and down the Walk, which is quite fun. It's a lot more of a relaxed restaurant and not suited to a huge crowd. But with just a few mates, it's a good night out.

4 BUFFET KING EDIN/LOTH
6a Nicolson Street, Edinburgh
0131 557 4567
A complete contrast to La Favorita, Buffet King is very suited to large groups of people scoffing their faces on a Friday lunchtime, with as many ribs, noodles and then ice-creams as physically possible. Definitely a good cheap way of getting loads of mates together, acting quite childishly, then going out to the cinema. A good fun way of spending an afternoon.

5 MOSQUE KITCHEN EDIN/LOTH
19a West Nicolson Street, Edinburgh
The mosque is easily one of the best places to have a curry in Edinburgh. For £3, you get a huge plate of lamb or chicken curry, with rice, and it is gorgeous. The tables are all outside with a canvas covering them, so wrap up warm if you go there at night. The place is always quite packed, but the queue goes down pretty quickly and the plates are all paper so you can leave with your meal.

51 GREAT ROADS FOR BIKERS

1 BEALACH NA BA HIGHLANDS
Tricky to name the actual road as it's a minor one heading east from Kishorn in Wester Ross. Take the A896 to Shieldaig and you'll see a sign to Applecross over the Bealach na Ba which means Pass of the Cattle. Low-key signage belies the fact this is one of Scotland's most famous roads and one of the most challenging you'll ever see. You climb more than 2,000 ft over five miles of switchbacks and steep climbs.

2 A82 GLENCOE OVER RANNOCH MOOR TO CRIANLARICH HIGHLANDS
This featured in the *Long Way Down* programme with Ewan McGregor and he said that he could feel the history bleeding out of the hills. It is a very atmospheric stretch, with wide open roads carving their way through towering mountains.

3 A832 KINLOCHEWE TO POOLEWE
HIGHLANDS
Loch Maree is thought of by many as one of Scotland's most beautiful, and the A832 hugs its shoreline to glorious Beinn Eighe – Britain's first nature reserve and home to a remnant of Caledonian Pine Forest. The views are mesmerising.

4 B8083, BROADFORD TO ELGOL ON SKYE HIGHLANDS

There are a few roads on Skye vying for a top spot, but the end result here is magical. The landscape changes frequently as the road fringes Loch Slapin from Torrin before rising rapidly towards Elgol. You're more likely to navigate around cattle than cars.

5 A84 CALLANDER TO ST FILLANS WHLLS&T

This might be cheating, as the A84 leads on to the A85 for St Fillans or takes you on to Killin – tough choice! The route has a fabulous mix of curves, scenery and changing landscapes, taking you past picture-postcard chalets in Strathyre and moody pine forests before Lochearnhead.

52 PRE-THEATRE MEALS

1 SISTERS RESTAURANT GLAS/CLYDE

36 Kelvingrove Street, Glasgow
0141 564 1157 *www.thesisters.co.uk*
Chic, sleek and contemporary, yet with a warm and friendly ambience. Three-course pre-theatre menu starts from £15 and includes a variety of dishes, locally sourced, seasonally inspired and resonating with traditional influences.

2 TEMPUS EDIN/LOTH

George Hotel, 19–21 George Street, Edinburgh 0131 240 7197
www.eh2tempus.co.uk
Metropolitan look as befits its location in the centre of town. The pale woods, abundance of greenery and classy lighting mean this is a sophisticated option. Unlike higher-end restaurants, there is an abundance of smaller dishes

and light bites as well as larger dishes. Also has an extensive wine list and cocktail menu – ideal if you are a larger group or want a more lively start to your evening.

3 LA PARMIGIANA GLAS/CLYDE

447 Great Western Road, Glasgow
0141 334 0686 *www.laparmigiana.co.uk*
Popularity among the Italian community in Glasgow is testament to authenticity of menu and cuisine. Opened by the Givanazzi family in 1978 and has maintained its place ever since as one of the city's favourite Italian eateries, with a relaxed and friendly atmosphere. Menu is broad and varied, and the wine cellar has a wide range of exceptional bins. Three-course pre-theatre menu starts from £15.50.

4 MARTIN WISHART EDIN/LOTH

54 The Shore, Edinburgh 0131 553 3557
www.martin-wishart.co.uk
Haven of contemporary chic and peace, with understated service and menu is so full of mouth-watering dishes, you won't be quite sure how on earth you will decide. Without a set pre-theatre menu, the à la carte menu, priced at £50, will mean having to eat quite quickly, so choose your dishes carefully – or it might be worth going to a matinée performance and having a post-theatre banquet.

5 THE PLUMED HORSE EDIN/LOTH

50–54 Henderson Street, Edinburgh
0131 554 5556 *www.plumedhorse.co.uk*
Two-course menu is priced at £31 and offers hungry theatre-goers the terrifying decision to choose between enticing delicacies that will tempt you to come back again and again.

53 TOYSHOPS

1 ABACUS WHLLS&T
The Arcade, Stirling 01786 478 784
Abacus in Stirling is a brilliant toy shop
– full of traditional toys that children
love. Their window display could rival
Hamley's, albeit on a smaller scale,
crammed full as it is of dolls' houses,
vintage pedal cars and knights' castles.
They also stock every kind of board
game, jigsaw and card game that an
adult could want.

2 THE SENTRY BOX GLAS/CLYDE
**175 Great George Street, Glasgow
0141 334 6070**
A treasure trove that harks back to a
more innocent age, stacked to the brim
with toy soldiers, wooden building
blocks, train sets and fairy costumes.
Has been delighting adults and children
alike for generations.

3 HARBURN HOBBIES EDIN/LEITH
**67 Elm Row, Leith Walk, Edinburgh
0131 556 3233**
This little toy and model shop on Leith
Walk is an Aladdin's cave of goodies,
from model railways and Scalextrix sets
to die-cast vehicles and Airfix kits.
There's plenty of interest for kids of all
ages (including adult ones) – from
Thomas the Tank Engine fans to serious
railway or military modellers, and the
friendly staff are always on hand with
helpful advice.

4 MUSEUM OF CHILDHOOD
**EDIN/LEITH 42 High Street, Edinburgh
0131 529 4142**
If you get through the gift shop
without forking out then you are
stronger willed than most. This isn't
because of pester power from the
youngsters, however – the cries of
recognition and excitement come from
the 30-plus brigade. Recall your youth
with a cylindrical box that moos when
you turn it over. Look out for pop guns
and Red Riding Hood dolls with granny
and the wolf hiding under her skirts.

5 THE HORSESHOE GALLERY SOUTH
**SCOT 22 Horsemarket, Kelso
01573 224 542**
Terrific selection of beautiful, authentic
toys in this Kelso gold mine, from
traditional bears to hand-crafted trucks
and children's games, some old, some
new, some just to look at but most to
play with, and all gift-wrapped. What
more could you ask for? Also great gifts
for older generations and good
selection of art work. Definitely worth a
look.

54 RUGBY GROUNDS

1 THE GREENYARDS SOUTH SCOT
Melrose RFC, Melrose 01896 822 993
www.melroserugby.bordernet.co.uk
Has few rivals for atmosphere and
beauty when bursting at the seams with
more than 12,000 people on Sevens day
in April – especially when the sun
shines. Nestled at the foot of the Eildon
Hills, it has a glorious view, the bankings
enclose the pitch neatly and the
modernised stand retains its traditional
charm. Inside, the club houses a unique
museum of rugby over the past 150
years. It's no surprise it attracts far-
travelled visitors all year round.

2 MURRAYFIELD *(when full)*
EDIN/LOTH
Scotland's top sports stadium remains
one of the most popular rugby venues
in the world for players and spectators

when it is full to capacity – modern, good walking space around perimeter inside and a terrific atmosphere, particularly when the Calcutta Cup is in town. Stark contrast when not full, and the distance the running track creates to the action is all too clear.

3 INVERLEITH EDIN/LOTH
Stewart's Melville RFC, Ferry Road, Edinburgh
A grand old dame of Scottish rugby, where Scotland played internationals in early 1900s, the great stand and views from Ferry Road across immaculate pitches and Edinburgh rooftops keep it among the gems of the game.

4 BURNBRAE GLAS/CLYDE
West of Scotland RFC, Burnbrae, Milngavie
There is an atmosphere about Burnbrae which smells of warm rugby hospitality – maybe that's just the whisky – and the upward climb of the 1st XV in recent times is bringing the crowds back to Milngavie. Not as swish as Old Anniesland, home of rival Glasgow Hawks, but the new stand has helped improve comfort and clubrooms retain unique character.

5 RIVERSIDE PARK SOUTH SCOT
Jedforest RFC
Sevens day in spring is best time to see this Jedburgh ground in all its glory, the bankings around the pitch filled with people and almost a circle of trees and the Jed Water enveloping them with a natural beauty. Hard to pick from age-old Borders grounds as they are all great theatres when housing a few thousand fans.

55 TOILETS

1 AUDI CAR SHOWROOM
GLAS/CLYDE A736, Junction 26 of M8, Hillington, Glasgow
The toilets in this glass complex rival, if not surpass, those at the Harvey Nichols store in Edinburgh – the Rolls-Royce of department store loos. They are ultra-modern with panelled walls, stylish basins and good lighting. The loos are just one unexpected aspect of the building which also includes a café, large children's play area and conference centre. You can buy a car too, if you like.

2 KYLE OF LOCHALSH HIGHLANDS
The public toilets in the town centre were one of the original 'pay-to-pee' loos and are clearly very well cared-for – very clean with real flowers. A very useful stop-off on a West Highland tour.

3 NATIONAL GALLERY OF SCOTLAND EDIN/LOTH The Mound, Edinburgh *www.natgalscot.ac.uk*
Beautiful oak doors, marble basins and slightly more spacious cubicles than modern loos. If you are ever stuck while shopping on Princes Street and need to spend a penny, this sure beats Jenners.

4 MOTHERCARE *all branches, www.mothercare.com*
This store cares about cleanliness for both you and your child. In addition, there is space for baby-changing gear, which is thoughtlessly absent in so many baby-change areas.

5 DUNKELD PAD&F
North car park, High Street
The newish loos at the north end of the High Street in lovely Dunkeld have

replaced those in The Square. They are modern, spacious and airy and one of the loos that charge where it is actually worth paying. Rail stations take note.

6 MUSSELBURGH EDIN/LOTH
Eskside East, off Shorthope Street
East Lothian has always had a good reputation for its public loos, and rightly so. These toilets just off Musselburgh High Street are beautifully clean and handy for shoppers and dog-walkers caught short (tie your dog up first – they aren't welcome inside).

56 SURFING BEACHES

1 BALEVULLIN BAY WHLLS&T
Isle of Tiree
www.adventure.visitscotland.com/ activities/water/surfing/
Not as famous as fabled point break at Thurso East, not as wild as some of the more terrifying big-wave spots on Lewis, but Balevullin is still the best place to go surfing in Scotland. Why? It's just plain magical. It is the most north-westerly of Tiree's many beaches and the prettiest. Blindingly white sand gives it a tropical feel, even in winter, and the water is startlingly green – and so clear you can almost always see the bottom. On big days, there are plenty of double-overhead barrels for local legends like Craig Sutherland to get swallowed up in, but even on a small swell the place is 100 different kinds of fun. Grab a longboard, paddle out and enjoy a mellow session with mellow locals who, in contrast to regulars at more crowded spots, will probably be happy to see you. That's another advantage about this place: it's so

remote that crowds are never really an issue. Even on the busiest days, there is always another stunning beach around the corner. None of this really does justice to the sheer magic of Balevullin. Maybe it's the resident seals who pop up to check out the action; maybe it's the walk through a cow field that reveals tantalisingly slowly what the waves are doing. Or maybe it's just the feeling this is the end of the line – about as far west as you can get, next stop America.

2 THURSO EAST HIGHLANDS
Caithness
Long, super-fast righthander that proved its world-class status in the O'Neill Highland Open. Top surfers just couldn't get enough of it.

3 PEASE BAY EDIN/LOTH
Near Cockburnspath, East Lothian
Discovered by pioneer Andy Bennetts in late Sixties and beloved of Edinburgh surfers ever since. Not a pretty beach, but the waves more than make up for the caravans.

4 SKATERAW EDIN/LOTH
Near Dunbar, East Lothian
Shallow reef break that hosted inaugural C2C Big Wave Challenge in November 2005. Needs a meaty swell to work. In shadow of Torness nuclear power station.

5 SANDWOOD BAY HIGHLANDS
Sutherland
It's a long, long walk to isolated Sandwood, but well worth it. Picks up pretty much any swell going. The four-and-a-half mile hike to Sandwood starts at Blairmore, north-west of the hamlet of Kinlochbervie on the single-track

B801. Just follow your nose. Perhaps the most inaccessible surf spot in mainland Britain, so rarely crowded.

6 BRIMS NESS BOWL HIGHLANDS
Near Thurso, Caithness

Scary, super-hollow hell-wave breaking onto a shallow, slate shelf. Picks up any swell going on the north coast, so if it's flat here, it's flat everywhere. Bring a helmet. Situated on Caithness's rugged north coast, just to the west of Thurso, the Brims consists of a huge rocky slab jutting out into the treacherous waters of the Pentland Firth. Access isn't too tricky – leaving Thurso you simply turn right off the A835 after about five minutes and drive through a farmyard to the break.

7 BELHAVEN BEACH EDIN/LOTH
Dunbar, East Lothian

Part of a nature reserve with two miles of golden sand, this beach is a large sandy crescent-shaped bay producing nice rolling waves north of Dunbar. It is a stunning location to learn to surf. The beach is used by several surf schools. Its neighbour, Pease Bay, just ten minutes south, is one of the best surf locations in Scotland but as a result very crowded. So if you are a beginner and don't need the crowd, go to Belhaven.

8 FRASERBURGH BEACH

ABER/GRAMP *(A90 south of Fraserburgh)* **Aberdeenshire**
The North East is blessed with hundreds of miles of uncrowded sandy beaches. Fraserburgh is the east coast's most consistent surfing zone with a swell window of almost 270 degrees.
The area is wide open to the small and medium-sized southerly and east swells

which are more of a summer occurrence.

9 EOROPIE OUT. ISLES
Lewis *(in the very north, drive up the A857 and off the B8013)*
The Hebrides are home to some of Europe's most consistent and powerful beach and reef breaks. With over 70 beaches throughout the Outer Hebrides, from white shell sands to pebble shores (and almost always empty), this really is surfer paradise. Eoropie has a very heavy beach break.

10 MACHRIHANISH WHLLS&T
Near Campbeltown, Mull of Kintyre
www.visitscotland.com/adventure
The long and narrow coastline of the Mull of Kintyre provides the best surfing on the south-west coast mainland where there is a small swell window between Ireland and Islay. This beautiful sandy beach is great for beginners as there are no reefs or rocks to wipe out on.

57 WALKERS' BARS

1 CLACHAIG INN HIGHLANDS
Glencoe 01855 811 252
www.clachaig.com
If there is a better located pub in Scotland than the Clachaig Inn, situated just off the A82 in Glencoe, most of us have yet to hear about it. After a day on the Aonach Eagach, either of the Buachailles, or Bidean nam Bian, the Clachaig is the perfect place to unwind and swap stories of derring-do on the mountains with fellow walkers. There are up to eight real ales available at any given time, including Fraoch from Heather Ales and at least one from Skye. There are beer festivals held

during the year when the number of real ales virtually doubles. The food is wholesome and hearty.

2 THE SLIGACHAN HOTEL
HIGHLANDS **Sligachan, Skye**
01478 650 204 *www.sligachan.co.uk*
No matter which of the Cuillin you attempt, from the comparatively straightforward ascent of Bla Bheinn (Blaven) to the seemly unclimbable Inaccessible Pinnacle on Sgurr Dearg, you deserve a pint on your return to sea level, where you started your walk. Taking localism as far (or near) as it can, the Cuillin Brewery is attached to the hotel and brews beers suitable for vegetarians and vegans.

3 THE GROG AND GRUEL
HIGHLANDS **66 High Street, Fort William**
01397 705 078
www.grogandgruel.co.uk
Ideally located for anyone who has tackled the Ben (only tourists call it Ben Nevis) or the Mamores from Glen Nevis. The Grog is a bare-boarded alehouse serving up to six real ales in summer and two or three in the off season. Beers often come from Isle of Skye and Heather Ales. As the name suggests, food is also a mainstay at the Grog, with chilli being a bit of a speciality. If doing the Ben, I would recommend that you combine it with Carn Mor Dearg from Glen Nevis, giving you the benefit of ascending the Carn Mor Dearg Arete and coming down the so-called tourist path.

4 THE GLENISLA HOTEL HIGHLANDS
Kirkton of Glenisla 01575 582 223
www.glenisla-hotel.com
On the B951 off the A93 Perth to Braemar road. It is fairly well placed for

refreshments after a day out on Glenshee, either tackling the long but fairly straightforward six Munros to the east of the Glenshee summit – including Tolmount and Tom Buidhe – or the far easier triple-header of the Cairnwell, Carn Aosda and Carn a'Gheoidh to the west of the summit. Please note that using the ski lifts is cheating. The range of real ales varies, but often includes beer from Inveralmond, in Perth, and Fyne Ales in Argyll. The food is more formal than the other recommendations and is restaurant food rather than pub grub.

5 THE ORMIDALE HOTEL SOUTH SCOT **Brodick, Arran 01770 302 293**
www.ormidale-hotel.co.uk
A trip here does not include Munro bagging, as there are no Munros on Arran. However, at a height of approximately 2,700 ft, Goat Fell is not too far short and, as you must start from virtually sea level, you will have far more ascent than many Munros. The Ormidale Hotel, on the northern outskirts of Brodick, just behind the golf course, is Arran's original real ale pub and now sells beer from the Arran Brewery through traditional Scottish air pressure tall founts.

58 WISHING WELLS AND TREES

1 ST CURITAN'S WELL HIGHLANDS
Munlochy, Black Isle, near Inverness
Named after a 7th-century Scottish missionary but probably much older than that. This is Scotland's best example of a 'clootie well', so-called because people tie cloth to surrounding trees in the hope of having a wish

fulfilled or something healed. This well, which lies about half a mile west of Munlochy in the Black Isle, is reached by stone steps. The well and surrounding trees are festooned with rags.

2 WISHING TREE WHLLS&T
Kilmelford *(on the A816 between Oban and Lochgilphead)*
This tree has been embedded with coins over many years. It is situated on a path up the Bealach Gaoithe above Armaddy Castle in Argyll. The tree itself is a hawthorn, an early blossoming tree that is held sacred in Celtic tradition and has associations with fertility. It is thought that removal of a coin from the tree will bring bad luck.

3 CLOOTIE TREE WHLLS&T
Aberfoyle, Trossachs
Located on Doon Hill and centred on an old pine tree. This tree is said to hold the spirit of the Reverend Robert Kirk, minister of the nearby Old Kirk of Aberfoyle. He was a seventh son, thought to have the gift of second sight. In 1691, he wrote a book called *The Secret Commonwealth*, an account of nature and society of the fairy world. From the village, walk up Manse Road, take the left fork after about ½ mile. This leads onto a forest track. Watch for the signs for Fairy Hill after about ¼ mile. At the top of the hill in amongst the trees you can see prayer ribbons that people still leave. When you reach it, hold hands around the tree, and circle it left three times, and right three times, make a wish, and don't tell anyone.

4 ST MARY'S WELL HIGHLANDS
Culloden
Named after a nearby chapel dedicated to St Mary and lying close to the

famous battlefield. It sits on an elevated plateau where a natural spring flows from a stone basin and it is surrounded by a low circular wall. This well is another example of a 'clootie well' and is said to be haunted by the ghosts of the fallen warriors of Culloden.

5 WISHING TREE HIGHLANDS
Loch Maree, near Kinlochewe, Wester Ross
This ancient oak tree is situated on Isle Maree, part of a small archipelago in Loch Maree. Both loch and island are named after the 7th-century saint Maelrubha, who is said to have founded a small church on the island, close to an ancient holy well. The tree is studded with coins and was visited by Queen Victoria in 1877.

59 FILM LOCATIONS

1 THE WICKER MAN SOUTH SCOT
Burrow Head, Dumfries & Galloway
Though set on a fictional Hebridean island, the cult thriller starring Edward Woodward and Christopher Lee was filmed in various locations across Scotland, including Skye, Plockton and Culzean Castle in Ayrshire. The bulk of filming, however, took place along the Solway coast of Dumfries & Galloway, including the iconic climax, in which Woodward's character is burned alive inside a giant pagan effigy. These scenes were filmed in the rather unlikely surroundings of a caravan park at Burrow Head near the Isle of Whithorn.

2 LOCAL HERO ABER/GRAMP
Pennan, Banffshire
The north-east port of Pennan, along with neighbouring Crovie, is one of the

most beautiful parts of the country. And it is impossible to talk about the tiny village, which nestles at the bottom of a plunging cliff road, without mentioning *Local Hero* in the same breath. Parts of the 1983 film starring Burt Lancaster were shot there – in particular the iconic scene featuring a red telephone box.

3 TRAINSPOTTING HIGHLANDS
Rannoch Moor

Although best-known as a gritty tale of urban squalor and drug addiction shot in Edinburgh, Glasgow and London, one of the movie's most memorable moments takes place when Renton, Spud, Sickboy and Tommy go for a day out in the Highlands. The sequence was filmed at remote Corrour Station in the middle of Rannoch Moor, which can only be reached by train on the Glasgow to Fort William line (see www.firstgroup.com/scotrail for train times). The toxic foursome don't get very far before Renton, played by Ewan McGregor, unleashes a bitter tirade about the crapness of being Scottish.

4 BRAVEHEART HIGHLANDS
Glen Nevis

While a deal of 1995's Mel Gibson kilts 'n' claymores epic was filmed in Ireland, much was shot in and around the tranquil Glen Nevis, including the scene where William Wallace takes his revenge on a fortified English garrison. The 'Braveheart Village' was left in situ after filming was completed, and became something of a shrine for nascent fans of the movie, but it is unlikely that anything now remains of the sets. Still, there's excellent winter walking in the area, and an out-of-season visit is heartily recommended for anyone wishing to unleash their inner Braveheart.

5 YOUNG ADAM EDIN/LOTH – GLAS/CLYDE The Forth and Clyde and Union canals

Fans of Alexander Trocchi's novel were divided by David Mackenzie's film adaptation, but the director certainly made a superb job of evoking the decaying industrial hinterland of post-war Scotland. Much of the action takes place aboard a canal barge skippered by Peter Mullan, on which Ewan McGregor takes refuge after the unfortunate death of his girlfriend. These scenes were filmed on both the Forth and Clyde Canal and the Union Canal. Thanks to the regeneration of the canals in recent times, the banks of either make for a pleasant stroll.

More info: www.scotlandthemovie.com

60 JAPANESE FOOD

1 OKO EXPRESS GLAS/CLYDE
80 Queen Street, Glasgow
0141 248 9666 *www.okoexpress.com*
Makes the packeted stuff you get in some high-street stores pale into insignificance. It works on a tapas basis, where you just pick and mix portions, and is better-suited for a quick lunch rather than a romantic meal for two. Best of all, the prices are good and it's open until 5am, Tuesday-Saturday, giving health-conscious clubbers an alternative to the kebab.

2 MISO GLAS/CLYDE
57 West Regent Street, Glasgow
0141 333 0133
Has a great atmosphere with a dark interior and fish tanks and a real Japanese feel. The quirky teriyaki boxes

on the menu have little compartments for very tasty treats, but being Glasgow, don't worry, you can have your sushi with chips. There's a good variety of cocktails and the bill won't break the bank.

3 YATAI ABER/GRAMP
53 Skene Street, Aberdeen
01224 658 521 *www.yatai.co.uk*
If you are looking for an authentic taste of Japanese cuisine in the North East, you can't get better than this relatively new restaurant. Aberdeen and nearby ports have built up an impressive reputation for seafood in most forms, but there are few places which serve it up raw. Yatai does so in delightful surrounding, and complements it with liberal helpings of sake and desserts such as green tea ice-cream.

4 BONSAI EDIN/LOTH
46 West Richmond Street, Edinburgh
0131 668 3847
www.bonsaibarbistro.co.uk
Brilliant range of authentic Japanese dishes at very good prices – and although it can be a wee bit cramped, this is part of its charm. Regular and loyal clientèle includes Japanese students from the university. Try the squid sprinkled with lemon and sea salt and the miso soup – and marinated octopus if you feel adventurous.

5 WAGAMAMA GLAS/CLYDE
97–103 West George Street, Glasgow
0141 229 1468
It might be part of a big chain, but it serves great Japanese food at very reasonable prices in an open modern environment. The Wagamama ramen is my favourite, and they do a decent kids' menu and take-away.

61 BIRTHPLACES TO VISIT

1 BURNS COTTAGE SOUTH SCOT
Alloway, Ayr 01292 443 700
www.burnsheritagepark.com
Burns was born in the cauld blasts of January 1759, in this thatched, whitewashed 'auld clay biggin' where he spent his first seven years. Nearby is the ruined Auld Kirk where Tam o' Shanter spied the witches and warlocks making merry. Behind the cottage is the leaking museum (open daily), which is being replaced by a more appropriate building for the 250th centenary of the Bard's birth.

2 JOHN MUIR HOUSE EDIN/LOTH
126 High Street, Dunbar, East Lothian
01368 865 899 *www.jmbt.org.uk*
The pioneering conservationist spent 11 years in Dunbar before emigrating to the US in 1849. He travelled, wrote and campaigned tirelessly to protect the wilderness as a space for spiritual refuge, and secured the Yosemite Valley in California as the first National Park. Muir is now celebrated in this fine museum (open April–October daily and November–March from Wednesday to Sunday). A two-mile clifftop walk leads to the John Muir Country Park.

3 HUGH MILLER'S COTTAGE
HIGHLANDS Church Street, Cromarty
01381 600 245 *www.hughmiller.org*
Cromarty consists of tiny whitewashed cottages and gems of Georgian architecture. It was in one of the former that Miller was born in 1802 – a stonemason who became a folklorist, self-taught geologist, prolific writer and journalist. The thatched cottage and

Miller House (open April to September daily; and in October, Sunday to Wednesday) show his possessions.

4 CARLYLE'S BIRTHPLACE SOUTH SCOT Ecclefechan, Dumfries 0844 493 2247 *www.nts.org.uk/Property/60/*

Thomas Carlyle, the Sage of Chelsea, voluminous writer on philosophy, politics, history and cultural criticism, was born in the modest Arched House (open June–September, Friday–Monday) in 1795. Hugely influential on Victorian politicians and reformers.

5 ANDREW CARNEGIE BIRTHPLACE MUSEUM PAD&F Moodie Street, Dunfermline, Fife 01383 724 302 *www.carnegiebirthplace.com*

Carnegie was born in a hand-loom weaver's cottage in 1835. The cottage (open April to October) charts his rise to American steel magnate. The richest man in the world when he sold out in 1901 to become a philanthropist.

62 SUNDAY LUNCHES

1 TULLIE INN WHLLS&T Fisherwood Road, Balloch Road, Balloch 01389 752 052

In its position next to Loch Lomond, The Tullie Inn is the ideal place to stop for Sunday lunch during a day of walking and sightseeing. There are a range of home-made dishes, with a strong Scottish theme. The decor is traditional, warm and welcoming, especially on those cold rainy days in the Trossachs. Originally built in 1895, the inn also includes a 12-room hotel

for those wanting to spend more time in the area.

2 URBAN ANGEL EDIN/LOTH 121 Hanover Street, Edinburgh 0131 225 6215 *www.urban-angel.co.uk*

Food is great, staff are friendly, decor is interesting (see their depictions of what urban angels might look like). Most importantly, the space is user-friendly – you may happily dine alone, with friends, parents, even your granny. This spot ticks all the right boxes for a Sunday lunch destination.

3 THE COMPASS BAR EDIN/LOTH 44 Queen Charlotte Street, Leith 0131 554 1979

Opens at 12:30 on Sundays with a hearty but high-quality menu guaranteed to see off a hangover. Relaxed, gastropub-style dining and entertaining staff. Easy to while away the entire afternoon here until you're ready to face that restorative pint or glass of wine come the early evening.

4 GREYWALLS EDIN/LOTH Gullane, East Lothian 01620 842 144 *www.greywalls.co.uk*

Ideal for Sunday lunch and a stroll on some of Scotland's best beaches. Built up an enviable reputation for great food and new head chef David Williams, previously at Michelin-starred restaurant Chapter One in Kent, secured this reputation, bringing a third AA Rosette in 2006. Grows his own veg and herbs, butchers his own meat.

5 EE-USK OUT. ISLES North Pier, Oban 01631 565 666

Spectacular view across Oban Bay to Kerrera and Mull and well-run with strong emphasis on good service.

Housed in a modern building, it is the best place to watch the buzz of the harbour. Huge range of locally sourced seafood including king scallops and oysters.

63 SMALL CINEMAS

1 GLASGOW FILM THEATRE
GLAS/CLYDE **12 Rose Street** (off Sauchiehall Street), **Glasgow**
0141 332 8128 *www.gft.org.uk*
The seats in this popular two-screen may not be as big and comfortable as those at the nearby Cineworld tower, but this is more than made up for by the wide range of home-grown and foreign films on offer. Several films include Q&As with actors and directors. Nowhere else could you see Kate Dickie, star of the award-winning Red Road, introduce the film on its first night. Also has a fine café (Cosmo) for pre- and post-film refreshment.

2 THE CAMEO EDIN/LOTH
38 Home St, Edinburgh
0870 755 1231/0131 228 2800
www.picturehouses.co.uk
Not only good for new indie films and vintage classics, but also for the excellent café which hosts themed music nights. Infectious enthusiasm for alt-arts lifestyle. Almost succeeds in making '80s casualties feel young again.

3 GROSVENOR CINEMA GLAS/CLYDE
Ashton Lane, Glasgow 0141 339 8444
www.grosvenorcinema.co.uk
This two-screen is a favourite with students and the 'cool set'. Comfortable seating, with the option to rent a sofa from which to enjoy the movie. More

mainstream offerings than many smaller cinemas, so popular with those who want to avoid the more tacky side to large film complexes. Close to West End's trendy bars/eateries.

4 MACROBERT ARTS CENTRE
WHLLS&T **University of Stirling**
01786 466 666 *www.macrobert.org*
An evening at the MacRobert is a great night out. Start with dinner and drinks in the relaxed (and cheap) café, before heading into the one-screen cinema for the main feature. Drinks at the bar are reasonably priced and you can take them into the film in plastic cups. Almost every showing is fully booked, mainly because the films are a carefully chosen mix of quality new releases and old classics.

5 NEW PICTURE HOUSE PAD&F
117 North Street, St Andrews
01334 474 902 *www.nphcinema.co.uk*
Mixing the old world charm of a small classic venue with some of the modern multiplexes, the NPH is an institution for students and locals. It has two smaller screens carved into the cavernous main screen so it can show more movies. The website is pretty good.

64 PLACES TO BUILD SANDCASTLES

1 ST ANDREWS EAST SANDS PAD&F
St Andrews, Fife
St Andrews is a popular visitor destination, and its beaches are one of the main reasons. For building sandcastles, the East Bay, lesser famed than West Sands, is best because it is

THE CAMEO 1 2 3
KISS KISS BANG BANG 15
BROKEN FLOWERS 15 CORPSE BRIDE
G HOST IN THE SHE LL 2 BATTLE IN HEAVEN 18
FRI LATE NIGHT RABID 15
trist
Dem
Barb
0131 466 32
www.demon-barber

more sheltered from the strong Scottish winds, meaning the castles last for longer. The wide range of facilities available makes East Sands an ideal venue for a fun family day out.

2 MAIDENS BAY SOUTH SCOT
Ayrshire *(near Turnberry, off A719)*
With the historic Culzean Castle nearby and Turnberry down the road, Maidens Bay is a very special sandcastle building spot in Scotland. The lovely long sandy beach and grass foreshore created perfect conditions for sand sculpting when the tide is on its way out after making the sand moist and damp. It was at Maidens that Robert the Bruce landed when he sailed from Rathlin Island.

3 EAST BEACH HIGHLANDS
Nairn, Moray
The East Beach, just past the Lochloy caravan park, in Nairn, is a great place to build your sandcastles. There are great views out across the Moray Firth and, when it's not covered in rain clouds, you can see the Black Isle. Nip back to the harbour for an ice-cream or just gather up the golden sands in your bucket and create a masterpiece.

4 ELIE PAD&F
East Neuk of Fife *(follow A917)*
The sands at Elie are perfect for making sandcastles, if the local cricket team are not playing beach cricket. The sands are sheltered and the sand is what you might call large-grained, which makes it easy to mould. Throughout summer, on most Sundays the welcoming local pub, the Ship Inn, runs an outdoor barbecue from 12.30 pm onwards. It's a great way to feed the family and enjoy a few cold beers on a sunny day – before going back to the sandcastles.

5 LONGNIDDRY BENTS, EDIN/LOTH
Longniddry, East Lothian
Not as immediately beautiful as the gorgeous yellow beaches of Gullane and Yellowcraigs, further down the coast, but much more fun. The damper sand is better for sculpting and the rocks and rockpools are fantastic for exploring and climbing. Also good for walking the dog.

65 CLIMBING FOR BEGINNERS

1 EDINBURGH INTERNATIONAL CLIMBING ARENA EDIN/LOTH
South Platt Hill, Newbridge, near Edinburgh 0131 333 6333
www.adventurescotland.com/
The biggest indoor climbing arena in the world, just outside Edinburgh, is perfect for learning to climb, with walls of all angles and sizes, and highly-qualified, experienced instructors to take you through the technicalities with all the safety equipment you need.

2 REIFF HIGHLANDS
near Ullapool
The idyllic sea cliffs north-west of Ullapool provide a beautiful and peaceful setting. The cliffs are never more than 25 m high so they provide a manageable introduction to climbing on sound, 'grippy' rock.

3 GLEN NEVIS HIGHLANDS
Minutes from Fort William, the numerous crags of Glen Nevis provide the biggest concentration of roadside climbing in Scotland. The climbs range from short 'boulder problems' to routes several rope lengths long which require

climbing belays or stops along the way up the cliff.

4 COIRE LAGAN HIGHLANDS
Skye

This impressive corrie hosts some amazing climbing around the Cioch, a huge perched block high up on the rock walls of the corrie, which provides a spectacular picnic ledge on the way up these cliffs. The gabbro rock the cliffs are made from is possibly the best you will ever climb on. People of a certain age might remember the Cioch from the epic sword fight between Sean Connery and Christophe Lambert in *Highlander* – those guys were brought in by helicopter though!

5 CENTRAL BELT CRAGS GLAS/CLYDE – EDIN/LOTH

This one is a bit of a cheat as it covers a big area, but the crags and quarries from Dumbarton in the West to Traprain Law in the East provide the perfect opportunity for the majority of the population to sample outdoor climbing on their doorstep. Some of them are prettier than others but if the climbing bug has bitten you won't mind as long as you can get climbing.

66 WATERSIDE WALKS

1 FALLS OF CLYDE GLAS/CLYDE
New Lanark 01555 665 262
www.swt.org.uk/wildlife/fallsofclyde.asp
Celebrated in art and literature, these are Britain's greatest falls. View after rain, when there's water to spare from the hydro-electric works. Start with the spectacular view overlooking the mills and village from the car park, then down

to the river and on to the three falls – Bonnington Linn, Cora Linn and Dundaff Linn. Watch the Clyde spating and spraying, rolling and roiling, rumbling and tumbling, frothing and flocculating.

2 RIVER DON ABER/GRAMP
Aberdeen

Short walk following the Don through Seaton Park, overlooked by the twin towers of St Machar's Cathedral. The river runs through a tree-hung gorge, past the restored old houses of Balgownie and under the ancient Brig o' Balgownie. Continue through Donmouth Local Nature Reserve and down to the sea, looking back to capture the brig framed by multi-coloured splashes of hazy foliage, like an impressionist sketch.

3 LOCH ACHRAY WHLLS&T
Aberfoyle, Trossachs

It's the wee loch between Venachar and Katrine, renowned for its reflections. Start at the viewpoint on the Duke's Pass Aberfoyle to Trossachs Pier road, then walk down to the lochside. Stroll along the watercolour gallery: trees and mountains painted on the canvas of the loch. Just stand there and reflect!

4 UNION CANAL EDIN/LOTH – GLAS/CLYDE

Linlithgow or Polmont to the Falkirk Wheel is great, but any rural section of the Union or Forth & Clyde canals will be fine. Autumn is undoubtedly the best time for toeing the towpath: the hedgerows are a cornucopia of fruitfulness, heaving with hips and haws, bursting with brambles, reddened with rowans, rich and ripe with multifarious seed-heads. Boats sailing, swans gliding, leaves drifting.

5 WATER OF LEITH EDIN/LOTH
Edinburgh
Try the section between the Gallery of
Modern Art and Canonmills. With luck,
Keats' 'conspiring sun' will be dappling
boughs and trunks and conjuring an
illuminated patchwork tapestry.
Canonmills is a gnat's leap from the
Botanic Gardens if you want to pop in.

67 BED AND BREAKFASTS

1 STRUAN HOUSE WHLLS&T
Harbour Street, Tarbert, Loch Fyne
01880 820 190 *www.struan-house-lochfyne.co.uk*
Simply fabulous. Situated right on the
harbour, it is decorated to a very high
standard with each of the rooms named
after Scottish islands. The owner is a
sculptor who skippered private yachts
for years, he tells great stories and
makes the best scrambled eggs ever.
All in all, a top place with superb
hospitality.

2 TANTALLON B&B EDIN/LOTH
17 Tantallon Place, The Grange,
Edinburgh 0131 667 1708
www.tantallonbandb.co.uk
Fantastic B&B within easy walking
distance of city centre in gorgeous
Victorian house run by lovely, friendly
couple. Breakfast is all organic and
cooked to perfection – not at all greasy.
Rooms are large, bright and spacious
and very clean. It is a delight to return
to this peaceful house after a busy day
in the centre and you are guaranteed a
good sleep!

3 WATER'S EDGE COTTAGE
WHLLS&T **Duck Bay, Arden,**

Loch Lomond 01389 850 629
www.watersedgecottage.co.uk
For a bit of romance, try Water's Edge
Cottage on the banks of Loch Lomond.
The breakfast is really good and the
owner operates an honesty bar – just the
ticket after a walk by the loch. The two
rooms in the cottage's eaves – 'Nook' and
'Cranny' – are beautiful and the views of
Loch Lomond from upstairs are great.

4 DROVERS' INN WHLLS&T
Ardlui, North Loch Lomond
01301 704 234
www.thedroversinn.co.uk
Has one of the most welcoming bars
and best breakfasts in Scotland.
A destination for those with a good
sense of humour and a love of
conversation, whisky and history. It is
also an excellent place for children;
imaginations will be stimulated by the
winding, crooked building, complete
with stuffed animals and ancient
armour. It is not, however,
recommended to anyone with Paris
Hilton tendencies.

5 ARDMORY HOUSE HIGHLANDS
Victoria Road, Fort William
01397 705 943
Good location, a warm greeting, clean
and comfortable rooms and a hearty
breakfast in the morning.

68 ROADSIDE FOOD

1 BALLINLUIG MOTOR GRILL PAD&F
Ballinluig, near Pitlochry 01796 482 212
*(100 m off the A9 Perth–Inverness road
20 miles north of Perth at the A827
junction)*
On the journey down the A9, stop off
at this award-winning café, a favourite
with long-distance lorry drivers and

tourists. The home-made soups are fantastic and the specials board is always a treat. There are also salads for those who want a lighter bite. The motor grill even accepts credit cards now.

2 HOT FOOD STAND AT THE TAY BRIDGE PAD&F

Customers can expect to be treated like royalty at this state-of-the-art hot food provider at the Fife side of the bridge. Service comes with a smile and a good Scottish slagging, overheard quotes include 'Eat your egg or wear it!' – but boy, the eggs are worth eating.

3 PIT STOP DINER WHLLS&T
The Pier, Arrochar 01301 702 570
Full of local atmosphere and international truckers, the Pit Stop Diner fills the hungry tums of drivers on the way down from Argyll. The diner is owned by the Arrochar and Tarbet Community Development Trust and received over £600,000 from the Big Lottery Fund to build three village halls. An experienced hill-walker, Craig Weldon, says: 'It's the best greasy breakfast in the land.'

4 BURGER VAN AT LOCH DOCHART
WHLLS&T *on A85*
The burger van at Loch Dochart is a true moveable feast, since it may not always be parked on the A85. But when it is, usually at the weekend, drivers are set for a gourmet treat. Serving specialities such as venison burgers, this is the nearest version of a Michelin-starred burger van that you will find.

5 THE HORN PAD&F
Errol, Perth 01821 670 237
Between Perth and Dundee on the A90,

this has the best bacon rolls in Scotland; you get about eight rashers of bacon per roll. They also do the sort of old-fashioned cakes and sweets that don't appear in up-market coffee shops. If you're after something even more substantial than their massive bacon rolls, they have a proper menu of caff-style grub too.

69 SHOE SHOPS

1 RUSSELL & BROMLEY GLAS/CLYDE
AND EDIN/LOTH **60 Buchanan St, Glasgow 0141 248 6031** *and* **106 Princes St, Edinburgh 0131 225 7444**
www.russellandbromley.co.uk
It was great news last year when Glasgow finally got a branch of R&B, as visiting this shoe shop is always the pinnacle of a high-street shopping experience. The foot candy is quite a bit more expensive than the usual fare but, if you've got a special occasion, it's worth splashing out on the leather finish, and the quality is outstanding.

2 SAM THOMAS ACCESSORIES
EDIN/LOTH **5 William St, Edinburgh 0131 226 1126**
This boutique is never as trend-led as high-street shops and has lots of classic styles in various colours. Handily, they're displayed on floor-to-ceiling shelves, making it easy to find what you want. Prices are always reasonable, starting from around £20 for a pair of ballet pumps.

3 HOUSE OF FRASER GLAS/CLYDE
21–45 Buchanan St, Glasgow 0870 160 7243
www.houseoffraser.co.uk
If you need a pair of everyday shoes, go to Office or Schuh but, for a really

special pair, visit the sprawling ground floor shoe department of Frasers in Glasgow. It's stuffed to the rafters with shoes by the likes of Gucci, Kurt Geiger and Bertie. They do a very good sale too, but sharpen your elbows.

4 PAM JENKINS EDIN/LOTH
41 Thistle St, Edinburgh 0131 225 3242
www.pamjenkins.co.uk
Be ready to spend lots of dosh on shoes by Christian Louboutin and Jimmy Choo, or just gaze in the window. If you're investing in a pair, then expect top-quality boutique treatment, comfy chairs, personal shopping with Pam herself – the works.

5 HELEN BATEMAN EDIN/LOTH AND HIGHLANDS **16 William St, Edinburgh 0131 220 4495** *and* **38 Union St, Inverness 01463 239 208** *www.helenbateman.com*
People return here again and again because of the great designs. The shoe-dyeing service is handy but the best thing about this shop is that – whether you buy zebra print pumps or court shoes – you are unlikely to be seen in the same shoes as anyone else.

70 PINE FORESTS

1 ABERNETHY FOREST RESERVE
HIGHLANDS **Central Highlands** *Grid Ref NH978183* **01479 831 476**
www.rspb.org.uk
At the northern end of the Cairngorms National Park, this is one of the largest wildlife reserves in Britain. The vast expanse of native pinewood supports pine marten, red squirrel, capercaillie, Scottish crossbill, crested tit and twinflower. Perhaps the best way to get an introduction to the area is to visit nearby Loch Garten Osprey Centre.

2 BEINN EIGHE NATIONAL NATURE RESERVE HIGHLANDS **West Highlands** *Grid Ref NH020630* **01445 760 254**
www.nnr-scotland.org.uk
Britain's first NNR (designated 1951) contains significant native pinewood, the largest of which is Coille na Glas Leitir (Wood of the Grey Slope). It has a different feel to east coast counterparts (perhaps because of high rainfall). One of the best places to see the elusive pine marten in natural surroundings.

3 BLACK WOOD OF RANNOCH
PAD&F **Perthshire** *Grid Ref NN617569*
www.forestry.gov.uk
On the southern shore of Loch Rannoch, this is part of the Tay Forest Park. Within the Forest Park there are a series of way-marked trails and picnic areas. In The Black Wood there are Scots pine that stood tall when wild boar, wolves and beaver roamed beneath them some 400 years ago.

4 GLEN AFFRIC NATIONAL NATURE RESERVE HIGHLANDS **Inverness-shire**
Grid Ref NH204235
www.nnr-scotland.org.uk
The largest surviving remnant of Caledonian pine forest outside of the Cairngorms National Park. Once heavily planted for commercial forestry, in the past couple of decades the Forestry Commission and Trees for Life have cleared large areas and allowed regeneration.

5 GLENMORE FOREST PARK
WHLLS&T **Central Highlands** *grid ref NH 978098* **01479 861 220**
www.forestry.gov.uk
The visitor centre, with audio-visual presentations and a café, is open all year. In addition to the usual pinewood

species, the prime location to see a rare species of wood ant. The narrow-headed ant is found here (and a few locations in Devon) and nowhere else in Britain!

71 CAMPSITES

1 CASTLE BAY SOUTH SCOT
Near Portpatrick, Wigtownshire
01776 810 462
www.castlebaycaravanpark.com
Caravan and campsite over 22 acres of rolling grassland atop towering cliffs, a short walk away from the picturesque village of Portpatrick. On a clear morning, you can unzip your tent to spectacular views over the water to the Emerald Isle. The site welcomes tents, touring caravans and also has a number of static caravans for rent. Open March to October.

2 OBAN CARAVAN AND CAMPING PARK WHLLS&T Gallanachmore Farm, Oban 01631 562 425
www.obancaravanpark.com
Covers 340 seaside acres, with magnificent views across the Sound of Kerrera. Pitches for tents and touring caravans, and also has a number of static vans for rent. Lovely rural setting, but just two and a half miles from Oban and a great base for exploring Argyll. There's a playpark and a duck-pond, too. Open end of March to October.

3 MORVICH CARAVAN CLUB SITE
HIGHLANDS Inverinate, Kyle
01599 511 354
Fantastically manicured caravan and campsite makes for a superb spot for a family holiday in the heart of walking country. Amid some of Scotland's most dramatic scenery, and much of the

surrounding land is owned by National Trust for Scotland. Guided walks throughout the season, so take walking boots. Open March to October.

4 BLAIR CASTLE CARAVAN PARK
PAD&F Blair Atholl, Perthshire
01796 481 263
www.blaircastlecaravanpark.co.uk
Award-winning, family-friendly site in the grounds of the famous castle. Consisting of more than 30 acres of parkland, the naturally terraced site is an excellent base for outdoor pursuits, especially walking, fishing, cycling and bird-watching. Caravan and tent pitches, as well as rentals. Open March to November.

5 BEINGLAS FARM CAMPSITE
WHLLS&T Inveranan, Dunbartonshire
01301 704 281
Friendly, reasonably-priced site half an hour's walk from Loch Lomond. Two good reasons to stay: if you want fun camping, hire a wigwam, and the site is a just a 10-minute stagger from one of the best places for a pint in Scotland – the Drovers Inn.

72 PLACES TO FIND CONKERS

1 LINN MILL EDIN/LOTH
South Queensferry
Follow signs for Hopetoun House from Bo'ness Road and turn into Hopetoun Road, which becomes Farquhar Terrace, then Society Road. Turn left on to Linn Mill and go up the hill. Swing right into an unnamed dead-end street and park carefully in front of the gate. Through the gate is a wide paved path, and on the right a stand of mature chestnut

trees. The trees grow on a lower level behind a wall, so branches are easy to reach. Follow the path for sweeping views of the Firth of Forth and Fife.

2 NEWHAILES ESTATE EDIN/LOTH
Musselburgh
Newhailes, the estate of the Dalrymple family, is a good place to take the kids and/or dogs, with lots of odd little pathways, strange architectural features such as the Shell House, sculptured benches, good berry-bushes and excellent sweeping views down to the Forth. And it's impossible not to find conkers.

3 SOUTHBRAE DRIVE GLAS/CLYDE
Jordanhill, Glasgow
Come out of Scotstounhill Station in Glasgow's West End, turn right and after the traffic lights, take the first right and you'll find yourself at the top of Southbrae Drive. Generations of pupils of Jordanhill School lucky enough to take this tree-lined route have arrived at school with pockets bulging with conkers. A tip for adult collectors – get there early to beat the kids.

4 HILLSIDE EDIN/LOTH
Edinburgh
London Road, heading out of town from Elm Row, is absolutely brilliant for conkers. On the hilly side, you'll soon get the additional delight of wading through wonderful swathes of knee-deep dead, dried leaves, corralled by the wind and perfect for running amok in – and not just if you're only 3 ft high.

5 BEVERIDGE PARK PAD&F
Abbotshall Road, Kirkcaldy
At the best of the Lang Toun's three huge public parks, start at the rugby clubhouse and head for the avenue of

trees that lead to the boating pond. There are enough chestnut trees to keep everyone happy. Take wellies if it's wet – there's no path.

73 EXTREME POINTS OF SCOTLAND

1 ARDNAMURCHAN HIGHLANDS
Ardnamurchan Lighthouse, built in 1849, is one of only four in Scotland – out of a total of 204 lighthouses – open to the public. It is close to the most westerly point on the British mainland, 22 miles further west than Land's End. The lighthouse was designed by Alan Stevenson, uncle of Robert Louis, and it is claimed to be the only lighthouse built in the Egyptian style.

2 MUCKLE FLUGGA OUT. ISLES
At the end of Unst in Shetland, these rocks were the most northerly inhabited place in the UK before automation of Muckle Flugga Lighthouse in 1995. It was engineered by Thomas and David Stevenson, father and uncle of Robert Louis Stevenson. Nearby Out Stack is Britain's most northerly dot of land, with nothing but water and ice between it and the North Pole.

3 BUCHAN NESS ABER/GRAMP
At the former fishing village of Boddam just south of Peterhead, this is one of Scotland's most easterly points. Buchan Ness Lighthouse (1827) was one of 18 designed by Robert Stevenson, grandfather of Robert Louis Stevenson.

4 DUNNET HEAD HIGHLANDS
This, not John o' Groats, is the northernmost point on the British

mainland. On the sheer sandstone promontory the Dunnet Head Lighthouse, 1831, designed by Robert Stevenson, stands 300 ft above the Pentland Firth. It has great coastal views and you can see across the sea to Orkney. The three-mile sandy beach of Dunnet Bay is popular with surfers.

5 MULL OF GALLOWAY SOUTH SCOT
South of Stranraer, with views of the Antrim Hills and the Mountains of Mourne, and situated in the mildest part of Scotland, this is its most southerly point. The Royal Society for the Protection of Birds has a nature reserve here, which is home to guillemots, razorbills and many other seabirds. Mull of Galloway Lighthouse (1830) is open to the public and was designed by Robert Stevenson.

6 SOAY OUT. ISLES
Excluding Rockall, the most westerly point of Scotland is the St Kildan isle of Soay, 110 miles west of the mainland. It is home to the small-bodied Soay sheep whose ancestors probably arrived in prehistoric times and now provide biologists with insights into evolution.

74 GREAT WEDDING LOCATIONS

1 BLUEBELL WOODS WHLLS&T
Balquhidder
Bluebell Woods is a popular spot for late-spring weddings, when the woodland floor is bright with flowers. Also in Balquhidder Glen, little Loch Doine, beside the larger waters of Loch Voil below the rugged Braes of Balquhidder, often has a similar role as a romantic backdrop.

2 THE HERMITAGE PAD&F
by Dunkeld, Perthshire
The Hermitage and Falls of Bruar are two scenic waterfall sites in a picturesque wooded gorge through which the River Braan plunges. Victorian folly Ossian's Hall is situated above the river and was built in 1758 to entertain visitors and provide spectacular views of the Falls of Braan, now owned by the National Trust for Scotland. The Falls of Bruar are a series of waterfalls eight miles from Pitlochry and have been a tourist attraction since the 18th century, famed for a connection to the poetry of Robert Burns.

3 SS *SIR WALTER SCOTT* WHLLS&T
Loch Katrine 01877 332 000 *(bookings)*
www.lochkatrine.com
The steamer the SS *Sir Walter Scott* has been sailing on Loch Katrine for more than a century and is named after the 19th-century novelist and poet who wrote 'The Lady of the Lake', and is the last of a series of ships to sail the loch. So why not become Lady of the Lake on your big day in the Trossachs?

Loch Katrine is 10 miles from Callander, via the A84 to Kilmahog, and the A821 through Brig o' Turk – or seven miles from Aberfoyle, via the A821 (Duke's Pass).

4 THE FALKIRK WHEEL WHLLS&T
Lime Road, Falkirk 01324 619 888
www.thefalkirkwheel.co.uk
The Falkirk Wheel is Scotland's unique revolving boat lift, and offers exclusive use of a private boat for a small gathering, or use of the space inside the main visitor centre. You can even have the colour scheme of your wedding projected up onto the wheel itself.

5 CAIRN GORM HIGHLANDS
www.cairngormmountain.org.uk
If you want to stage the highest wedding in the UK, Cairn Gorm will fit the bill. Travel up to the top by the funicular railway – you can even have your ceremony performed on the train. At the top you will find the highest restaurant and function venue in Scotland (the Ptarmigan – 01479 861336), with panoramic views and an outdoor terrace where your ceremony can be performed against a stunning backdrop of lochs and mountains.

6 ST SALVATOR'S CHAPEL PAD&F
St Andrews University, North Street
01334 462 226 *www.saint-andrews.co.uk/Tour/chapel.htm*
The chapel is available for weddings only to people who can prove a connection to the university or those living in a KY16 postcode, but tracking down a great aunt who once worked in the student canteen is worth it. The 15th century chapel has beautiful stained glass windows and guests spill out onto the picturesque university quadrangle afterwards. If it rains, pictures can be taken in stone-arched cloisters.

7 DUNKELD CATHEDRAL PAD&F
Cathedral Street, Dunkeld
01350 727 688 *(tourist information)*
www.dunkeldcathedral.org.uk
A wonderful building in a stunning location at the heart of the restored village, set in grounds that gently sweep down to the River Tay. With the nave an unroofed ruin, the current church occupies the remaining choir section, the perfect size for housing wedding guests in a dramatic space without swamping them with its scale.

Dunkeld House Hotel, just upstream, provides an ideal accompanying reception venue, reached via an imposing mile-long drive.

8 FALKLAND PALACE PAD&F
Falkland, Cupar, Fife 0844 493 2186
www.nts.org.uk
Beautiful, olde-worlde interiors give a classy and timeless feel, while the huge and delightfully landscaped gardens are perfect for enjoying a glass of champagne and a bite to eat before or after the service.

9 DRYBURGH ABBEY SOUTH SCOT
St Boswells, Melrose, Scottish Borders
01835 822 261 *www.dryburgh.co.uk*
Although ruined by the English in 1385, the walls and grounds are beautifully maintained and it is possible to hold a wedding within. The abbey, on the banks of the Tweed, is the perfect setting for great wedding pictures. The Dryburgh Abbey Hotel right next door is superb for a reception too, with exquisite food, great rooms and very hospitable staff. The famous Scott's View (of the Eildon Hills) is five minutes up the road, and another wedding photo opportunity.

10 AT SEA
The more romantic among us may choose to get married at sea. Any old skipper won't do – you must find a registered captain. A wedding on a boat guarantees a private, memorable day.

For more information, go to www.visitscotland.com/scottishwedding

75 AFTERNOON TEAS

1 BOLLINGER BAR PALM COURT AT THE BALMORAL EDIN/LOTH
1 Princes Street, Edinburgh 0131 556 2414 *www.roccofortehotels.com*
Take a Tardis time-trip to the 1920s and enjoy afternoon tea at the Bollinger Bar Palm Court at the Balmoral. High tea is served daily between 2.30 – 5.30 pm with linen napkins, French fancies and classic cucumber sandwiches, with harp music and 'Famous Edinburgh' tea.

2 THE HOWARD EDIN/LOTH
34 Great King Street, Edinburgh 0131 557 3500 *www.thehoward.com*
Invented by the 7th Duchess of Bedford to stop her hunger pangs between lunch and dinner back in the 1800s, afternoon tea is the perfect treat – and at the Howard, it is a splendid affair. Your designated butler will serve delights such as chocolate and hazelnut choux buns, home-made scones with clotted cream and preserves and spiced fruit palmiers with vanilla Chantilly cream.

3 CENTOTRE EDIN/LOTH
103 George Street, Edinburgh 0131 225 1550 *www.centotre.com*
If your mum liked *Ab Fab*, knows who Christian Dior was and wears Manolo Blahnik heels, then this is the afternoon tea location for her. With huge spacious interiors, clean white lines and minimalist furniture, Centotre is a fashionista hang-out. It also has very good cakes.

4 FIFI AND ALLY GLAS/CLYDE
51–52 Princes Square, Glasgow 0141 229 0386 *and* 80 Wellington Street, Glasgow 0141 226 2286 *www.fifiandally.com*
Since opening in 2005, Fifi and Ally has become a Glasgow institution for any lady who lunches. It's an amazing mix of shopping, food and fun. Everyone leaves Fifi and Ally smiling and feeling uplifted. In 2007 they had so many smiling customers at their Princes Square store that they opened a second café in Wellington Street.

5 KEMBER AND JONES GLAS/CLYDE
134 Byres Rd, Glasgow 0141 337 3851 *www.kemberandjones.co.uk*
K&J is a fine-food emporium, a magical place full of great-tasting food. There is no official serving time of afternoon tea, you can enjoy it all day long. Opened in 2004 by Claire Jones and Phil Kember, this brilliant café is always busy and bustling. Try a slice of pistachio, cardamom and orange tart, or maybe a piece of espresso, hazelnut and walnut cake.

76 FLORISTS

1 STEMS EDIN/LOTH
22–24 Grindlay St, Edinburgh 0131 228 5575 *www.stems.org*
Katrina Howells is one of the best florists in the capital. Her displays are always stunning and if you have an eye for interior design, this is the bouquet boutique for you. Located by the Lyceum Theatre, Katrina and her team can easily deliver throughout the city. Stems specialises in arrangements with provided vases which will be collected a fortnight later.

2 ROOTS AND FRUITS GLAS/CLYDE
351 Byres Rd, Glasgow 0141 339 5164 *www.rootsandfruits.co.uk*

Roots and Fruits first opened its doors in 1988, promising 'the freshest natural produce direct to the public'. Garth Gulland is the entrepreneur behind the business. It is his dedication and ability to pick the best seasonal flowers that make his empire the flower leader of Glasgow today. Along with the gorgeous flowers, Roots and Fruits also specialises in organic and wholefoods.

3 FLOWERS BY MONICA HIGGINS

EDIN/LOTH **22 Argyle Place, Edinburgh 0131 477 2923**
www.flowersbymonicahiggins.co.uk
Monica Higgins is the most internet- and photo-savvy florist in the capital. Her website is full of information and her flowers are outstanding. She really does say it with flowers. From a fragrant vase for the hall to something delicate for the dressing table, Monica provides the freshest and most unique bouquets.

4 LILIUM EDIN/LOTH

5a William St, Edinburgh 0131 226 4999
www.liliumflorist.co.uk/index.html
Nestled in fashionable William Street, Lilium provides a traditional service, specialising in roses. This flower boutique will make the recipient feel special and loved with their handcrafted traditional bouquets.

5 GLORIOSA EDIN/LOTH

46 Main Street, Davidson's Mains, Edinburgh 0131 336 1848
www.gloriosaflorist.co.uk
Gloriosa is owned and run by highly experienced florist Katherine Forsyth. Provides an alternative to the city-centre florists with no compromise on style or freshness. Clients include Sir Cliff Richard, the Dalai Lama and Sir Tom Jones.

77 PLACES TO SEE AUTUMN LEAVES

1 DUNKELD–BIRNAM PAD&F

Perthshire
The densely wooded hills and crags of this part of Perthshire have inspired such diverse literary icons as Shakespeare and Beatrix Potter. They are criss-crossed by a network of footpaths and cycle trails that really come into their own in the autumn. A stunning backdrop to the beautiful twin villages of Birnam and Dunkeld.

2 DALKEITH COUNTRY PARK

EDIN/LOTH **Dalkeith, Midlothian 0131 654 1666**
www.dalkeithcountrypark.com
Close to Edinburgh's city bypass, these woods were planted in the 1700s as part of an extensive pleasure garden around Dalkeith House. They now have a semi-wild feel, but don't worry – a ranger service is on hand to guide you through. This is the place to come to be buried in autumn leaves.

3 CAWDOR BIG WOOD HIGHLANDS

Cawdor Castle, Nairn, near Inverness 01667 404 401 *www.cawdorcastle.com*
In the grounds of Cawdor Castle, this is possibly the finest broad-leaf wood in the north-east of Scotland, with birch, beech, oak and rowan as well as a profusion of flora and fauna. The woods were originally planted in the 16th century.

4 DAWYCK BOTANIC GARDEN

SOUTH SCOT **Stobo, near Peebles, Scottish Borders 01721 760 254**
www.rbge.org.uk
This arboretum forms part of the Royal Botanic Garden Edinburgh group, which

took over the garden from its private owner in 1978. It has been an arboretum since it was planted out by the Veitch family in the 17th century. The autumn highlight is undoubtedly the fantastic beech avenue which runs up the valley of a beautiful hillside stream.

5 MOREBATTLE CHURCH SOUTH SCOT near Kelso, Roxburghshire
The graveyard of this 18th-century church is great for autumn leaves. It has a peaceful and idyllic location nestled in the heart of rolling Borders countryside that probably hasn't changed much for hundreds of years, other than the draining of the mere that gave Morebattle its name.

78 INDIAN FOOD

1 KHUSHI'S EDIN/LOTH
9 Victoria Street, Edinburgh
0131 220 0057
A family business that has survived six decades and, although there have been changes in location and decor and a few additions to the menu, one thing has remained consistent – the hearty welcome extended by the family. It is particularly known for its bhuna, an old family recipe which has grown in popularity over the years. If you are looking for good authentic Indian cuisine and a warm welcome, it has to be Khushi's.

2 MOTHER INDIA'S CAFÉ
GLAS/CLYDE 1355 Argyle Street, Glasgow 0141 339 9145
Mother India has developed a winning formula – fresh, delicious Indian food in a tapas format. Result – the right amounts of a range of flavours and textures. You feel pleasantly full with

none of the undesirable repercussions of an all-you-can-eat buffet. The food is freshly sourced and freshly prepared, and the service is friendly and reliable. An added bonus is the fact that you can combine a lunchtime curry with a visit to the Kelvingrove Museum and Art Galleries to make a perfect day out.

3 KALPNA EDIN/LOTH
2–3 St Patrick Square, Edinburgh
0131 667 9890
www.kalpnarestaurant.com
Delicious vegetarian food with delicate and surprising flavours and friendly, relaxed service. Excellent lunchtime buffet, with a changing variety of dishes. In the evening a good choice is a thaali – a platter offering a selection of curries, daal, raita and rice, with a desert as well. Vegan meals are also available.

4 KEBAB MAHAL EDIN/LOTH
7 Nicolson Square, Edinburgh
0131 667 5214
The tables are made of Formica and there is one of those dreadful dripping kebab monsters twirling in the window. But there is a reason why the Kebab Mahal is always packed full of happy punters and in the evenings often has a queue stretching out into the street. Authentically spicy curries, freshly grilled lamb and chicken and the softest, most sumptuous naan bread in town makes this Southside curry house a culinary delight.

5 INDIA QUAY GLAS/CLYDE
181 Finnieston Street, Glasgow
0141 221 1616
Glasgow's new premier Indian restaurant, opened in October 2005, offers quality northern Indian food.

All tables look out over the Clyde. Offers a select minimalist menu focusing on innovative creations providing meat and vegetarian options, which are beautifully presented and expertly prepared.

6 BALAKA PAD&F
3 Alexandra Place, Market Street, St Andrews 01334 474 825
Award-winning restaurant in the heart of St Andrews that has operated for 25 years under the watchful eye of Mohammed Abdur Rouf. The land at the back of the restaurant covers about an acre and is used for growing herbs and vegetables for the kitchen.

79 FAMOUS TREES

1 FORTINGALL YEW PAD&F
Fortingall Churchyard, Perthshire
www.forestry.gov.uk/forestry/ INFD-6UFC5F
Europe's oldest tree, the Fortingall Yew in Perthshire, is probably Scotland's most famous tree. In a graveyard in Fortingall village, various estimates have aged the tree at between 2,000 and 5,000 years. Because of tourist vandalism (cutting out small pieces of the tree to keep as a memento) and a little natural decay, the massive trunk of the Fortingall Yew has split into many sections. This gives the impression of multiple trees that are joined as one at the base.

2 CATACOL WHITEBEAM SOUTH SCOT **Arran**
www.rbge.org.uk/science/conservation
The Catacol whitebeam is Scotland's rarest tree, with only two mature examples. In fact, the tree grows only on Arran, but there are conservation

moves to protect and encourage small saplings by Edinburgh's Royal Botanic Garden. The Catacol whitebeam was named after the glen in which it was found, and its Latin name is *Sorbus pseudomeinichii.*

3 THE WISHING TREE HIGHLANDS
Kilmelford *(on the A816 between Oban and Lochgilphead)*
The wishing tree is totally unique. Presently fenced in to protect it, this hawthorn tree has been the wish-keeper of hundreds of dreams made in Scotland by visitors and locals alike. The Celts regarded hawthorns as sacred and marked their wishes by reciting the wish or prayer by the tree then embedding a coin in the bark. Prayers and wishes were offerings to the spirits and fairies that would either convey the wish to a higher authority or possibly grant it themselves.

4 THE MIGHTIEST CONIFER
WHLLS&T **Ardkinglas Woodland Garden, Cairndow, Argyll 01499 600 261**
www.ardkinglas.com
The conifer in Ardkinglas Woodland Garden was selected as one of 50 Great British Trees to celebrate Queen Elizabeth's Golden Jubilee. The trunk measures about 31 ft. The garden also has one of the tallest trees in Britain, a Grand Fir standing more than 200 ft tall.

5 ROBERT THE BRUCE YEW
WHLLS&T **Inchlongaig, Loch Lomond**
The yew is believed to have been planted by Robert the Bruce. In 1306, it became inextricably linked to him when he used it to rally his twice-defeated army after it escaped from the western to the eastern shore of the

loch. In 2003, it was revealed the tree was badly decayed inside and moves were made to let more light in to help save it.

80 VEGETARIAN RESTAURANTS

1 DAVID BANN EDIN/LOTH
56–58 St Mary's Street, Edinburgh 0131 556 5888 *www.davidbann.co.uk*
Vegetarians were expected to slum it before the advent of David Bann's upmarket restaurant. Everything on the menu is surprising, thanks to a few international influences. They know how to prepare polenta, tofu and couscous without creating a soggy, flavourless mass and always use a great range of seasonal vegetables and the best-quality ingredients.

2 SUSIE'S DINER EDIN/LOTH
51–53 West Nicolson Street, Edinburgh 0131 667 8729
A no-frills, canteen-style diner, where you pay for the plate size (about £6 for a big one) and the staff heap it high with treats like veggie enchiladas and interesting salads. And the cakes are great.

3 THE BAKED POTATO SHOP
EDIN/LOTH 56 Cockburn Street, Edinburgh 0131 225 7572
Sells the best potatoes ever. Forget puny tatties – these are extreme mutants that probably weigh the same as your head. Challenge yourself to eat a whole one. Fillings range from standard cheesy beano to interesting concoctions of kidney beans and tofu. You can get generous helpings of the salads to take away in a cup, useful

as there's only seating for four in the shop.

4 MONO GLAS/CLYDE
King's Court, 103 King Street, Glasgow 0141 553 2400
This place is a hang-out for trendy vegans who like to quaff organic beer from the Mono drinks menu and browse the adjacent record shop. It's cheap, cheerful in a bistro style, boasts some unique ways of preparing veg, great mezze and snack food and gets ethical points for supporting Fair Trade.

5 TCHAI OVNA GLAS/CLYDE
42 Otago Lane, Glasgow 0141 357 4524 *www.tchaiovna.com*
The Tchai Ovna house of tea does have hippy inclinations, but overlook those because the food is so darn good. It tastes healthy and wholesome. Choose from things like hearty chilli, tagine or dhal. You have to have a cup of their speciality teas to wash those legumes down, or even have a puff on their flavoured Shishah pipe.

81 CONTEMPORARY BUILDINGS

1 GARDEN PLANT EXHIBITION HOUSES EDIN/LOTH
Royal Botanic Garden, 20A Inverleith Row, Edinburgh 0131 552 7171 *www.rbge.org.uk*
Who says all 1960s buildings are ugly? The design problem here was to construct a building whose structure must not intrude into the interior. Created by a Scottish Office team led by George Pearce and built of steel and glass, this giant fairy tale structure blends in well with its pastoral

surroundings despite its size, while inside visitors can travel from jungle to desert.

2 ST BRIDE'S RC CHURCH

GLAS/CLYDE **Whitemoss Avenue, East Kilbride 01355 220 005**
Post-war Scotland is internationally famous for producing architecture that was uncompromisingly artistic and romantic. Witness the series of churches produced by the practice of Gillespie, Kidd & Coia, of which St Bride's is the most famous. Here, within an apparently windowless brick interior, there are no fewer than six concealed light sources.

3 THE BURRELL GLAS/CLYDE

Pollok Country Park, 2060 Pollokshaws Road, Glasgow 0141 287 2550
www.glasgowmuseums.com
The result of an architecture competition in 1971, the Burrell restored Glasgow's reputation for quality architecture, not to mention its tourism potential. Avoids the in-your-face super-modernism of later galleries and harks back to a more restrained – and pleasing – Scottish tradition. It is a gallery that shows off its contents rather than itself.

4 FALKIRK WHEEL & VISITOR CENTRE WHLLS&T **Lime Road, Falkirk 08700 500 208**
www.thefalkirkwheel.co.uk
The world's only rotating boatlift, used to connect the Forth & Clyde and Union canals, some would argue it is more sculpture than building. However, the thousands of visitors who flock to see it don't care. Designed by RMJM of Scottish Parliament fame (or infamy)

the Wheel has become an icon for Scottish architecture and tourism – and a good day out.

5 DUNDEE CONTEMPORARY ARTS,

PAD&F **152 Nethergate, Dundee 01382 909 900** *www.dca.org.uk*
By the time Dundee got round to trying to regenerate itself through art and architecture in the late 90s, the idea seemed old hat. But Richard Murphy's DCA put the city on the cultural map. Fusing new build and restoration, it marked a turn away from the contemporary fad of knocking everything down and starting again – and showed that successful modern architecture does not need to shock.

6 SCOTTISH PARLIAMENT

EDIN/LOTH **Holyrood, Edinburgh 0131 348 5000** *or* **0845 278 1999**
www.scottish.parliament.uk
The horrendous bill and thought of what talents like Frank Gehry or Zaha Hadid could have made with £430 million make it tempting to leave out the parliament. But the late Enrique Miralles' creation is notable for the debating chamber with its suspended beams, and the unforgettable flying ceilings of the committee rooms. The 'upended boats' design and landscaping are best seen from Arthur's Seat.

7 MAGGIE'S CENTRE PAD&F

Ninewells Hospital, Tom MacDonald Avenue, Dundee 01382 496 384
www.maggiescentres.org.uk
Overlooking the Tay Estuary, Frank Gehry's first building in Britain is a visual antidote to the looming greyness of Ninewells Hospital. The white tower of the cancer comfort centre is inspired by lighthouses, while the folded roof of

pine and plywood is finished in stainless steel. Inside, the spaces are equally light and uplifting.

8 DANCE BASE EDIN/LOTH
14–16 Grassmarket, Edinburgh 0131 225 5525 *www.dancebase.co.uk*
Architect Malcolm Fraser's latest showcase is the Scottish Storytelling Centre in the Royal Mile. But Dance Base is the old favourite, alive with energy, where visitors access the airy studios via ramps along old stone walls, with glimpses of dancers through opaque glass floors or roof walkways.

9 RADISSON SAS HOTEL GLAS/CLYDE
Argyle Street, Glasgow 0141 204 3333 *www.radisson.com*
The 250-bed hotel in Argyle Street is a much-admired Glasgow landmark, thanks to its dramatic curved copper screen. Gordon Murray and Alan Dunlop Architects used the green patina of the 'indigenous' copper and a glass bridge inside to break away from a mass-production, corporate hotel.

10 THE LOTTE GLOB HOUSE
HIGHLANDS **105 Laid, Loch Eriboll, Durness, Sutherland**
www.scottisharchitecture.com/article/view/Lotte+Glob+House
The two-storey house by architect Gokay Deveci, elevated on a slope overlooking Loch Eriboll, was designed to give ceramic artist Lotte Glob both studio and living space. It has a curved roof clad with patinated copper sheets, walls of untreated Scottish oak and a projecting timber deck. It must withstand the fiercest of winter winds.

82 SPORTS SHOPS

1 RUN AND BECOME EDIN/LOTH
66 Dalry Rd, Edinburgh 0131 313 5300 *www.runandbecome.com*
A compact, friendly store that caters only for runners. The patient staff, all pavement-pounders themselves, really know their subject. What's more, they will let you run a short distance up the street to try out shoes and they don't laugh at irrelevant questions, like 'How do you pronounce Saucony?' The flyers about forthcoming road races are useful, too.

2 THE TRIATHLON CENTRE
EDIN/LOTH **57–59 South Clerk Street, Edinburgh 0131 662 8777**
www.thebicycleworks.co.uk/triathlon
Run by Andrew Davies and John Anderson, the brains behind Edinburgh's popular Bicycle Works and both champion cyclists. The knowledgeable assistants will get you kitted out comfortably for running, cycling and swimming. The store even offers wetsuits for hire and a discount off the hire fee if you chose to buy it.

3 COW CORNER EDIN/LOTH
90 Brunswick Street, Edinburgh 0131 557 5070 *www.cowcc.com*
Scotland's only dedicated cricket shop is in Edinburgh and is owned by a couple of cricket enthusiasts. Friends who play say it's a great wee place, with friendly staff who play the game and who are very knowledgeable about the equipment and always keen to chat about the game.

4 RUN 4 IT ABER/GRAMP
21 Holburn St, Aberdeen *(also in Glasgow and Edinburgh)* **01224 594 400**

www.run-4-it.com
The Scottish chain that caters for everyone from recreational joggers to track athletes and triathletes. Helpful assistants will send you on to the streets with trainers so comfortable they could be tailor-made. Also offers a huge range of running gear for all weathers and handy accessories. Also a great place to pick up tips and information on forthcoming races and fun runs.

5 SWEAT SHOP *stores in* **Dundee, Edinburgh** *and* **Glasgow**
www.sweatshop.co.uk
Its staff are knowledgeable, both about their wide range of products and sports in general, and are happy to help.

83 FAIRTRADE CLOTHES

1 BOLSHIE GLAS/CLYDE
57 Bank Street, Glasgow 0141 357 1777
www.bolshieclothing.com
At the moment, you'll have to visit the Glasgow store to check out Bolshie's fantastic range of recycled, ethical and Fairtrade clothing and accessories, but an online store is in the pipeline. Among the wares on display are some rather fetching climate-change pants from Green Knickers that change colour with body heat, and gorgeous natural-fibre dresses by Sarah Ratty's Ciel label. www.greenknickers.org

2 SEESAW EDIN/LOTH
109 Broughton St, Edinburgh
0131 556 9672 *www.seesawtoys.co.uk*
For your mini eco-warrior, Seesaw sells adorable children's lines from Frugi and Green Baby, including 100 per cent

organic cotton babygrows manufactured in India on Fairtrade projects – give Gywneth Paltrow a run for her money...

3 dotRUN EDIN/LOTH
Studio G26, 32 Dalmeny Street, The Drill Hall, Edinburgh *www.dotrun.co.uk*
Quirky range of men's and women's hand-screen-printed T-shirts on American Apparel tees. Featuring hula-hooping street signs, retro details and motifs inspired by the designer's 'technical drawing days', they're sweat-shop free and just a little bit different.

4 ONE WORLD SHOP GLAS/CLYDE
100 Byres Rd, Glasgow 0141 357 1567
www.oneworldshop.co.uk
Bit of a one-stop shop for all your Fairtrade needs. As well as stocking food, jewellery and gifts, they have a great range of good-quality ethically sound clothing for men and women from labels such as People Tree, Traidcraft and Bishopton Trading.

5 MARKS & SPENCER
www.marksandspencer.com
Even M&S has got in on the game – the high street does a range of basic women's Fairtrade cotton T-shirts which come in a range of styles and colours, so now there's no excuse not to make ethically produced fashion a staple of your wardrobe. These are not just Fairtrade clothes, these are M&S Fairtrade clothes.

84 DAYS OUT ON ROYAL DEESIDE

1 VICTORIAN HERITAGE TRAIL
ABER/GRAMP **01339 755 306**
www.aberdeen-grampian.com

Follow in Queen Victoria's footsteps on the trail, which leads to some of the sights she enjoyed during her visits, including the Old Royal Station (Station Square, Ballater) which now houses a life-size Victorian railway carriage. The royal saloon carriage, as used by Her Majesty between Ballater and Windsor in the late 19th century, has been craned into the Old Royal Station, now a Tourist Information Centre and visitor attraction.

2 BALMORAL CASTLE ABER/GRAMP
Balmoral, Ballater, Aberdeenshire 01339 742 534
www.balmoralcastle.com
Purchased by Victoria in 1848, the estate has been the Scottish home of the Royal Family ever since. The estate extends to just over 50,000 acres of heather-clad hills, ancient Caledonian woodland, policies and the beautiful River Dee is nearby.

3 ROYAL LOCHNAGAR DISTILLERY
ABER/GRAMP **Balmoral, Crathie, Ballater, Aberdeenshire 01339 742 273**
www.visitscotland.com
Take a guided tour of this traditional working distillery, where you can see the distillers tending to the traditional mash tun and gleaming copper stills. You will see age-old traditions and craftsmanship in practice to produce one of Scotland's most exclusive whiskies.

4 CRATHES CASTLE ABER/GRAMP
Banchory, Aberdeenshire 01330 844 525
www.nts.org.uk
King Robert the Bruce granted the lands of Leys to the Burnett family in 1323; the ancient Horn of Leys, which can be seen today in the Great Hall,

marks his gift. A visit is enhanced by the walled garden, providing a wonderful display at all times of the year. The great yew hedges date back to 1702.

5 DEESIDE ACTIVITY PARK
ABER/GRAMP **Dess, Aboyne, Aberdeenshire 01339 883 536**
www.deesideactivitypark.com
The whole family can enjoy the pleasures of the active outdoors in 100 beautiful acres. Qualified instructors will always be on hand to make sure you get the most out of your visit, whether it's a lesson in kart racing, mountain biking or archery.

85 WATERCOLOUR ARTISTS

1 JENNY MATTHEWS 0131 441 2620
www.jennymatthews.co.uk
Successful artist for 20-plus years who counts Ian Rankin as a fan. Won a 2007 prize at a Royal Watercolour Society competition. Her inspiration is from painting flowers. A frequent visitor to the Royal Botanic Garden, complete with sketch book, in spring she is found in neighbours' gardens painting tulips and irises.

2 SUSAN MITCHELL 01721 723 385
Peebles-based full-time watercolour artist and etcher who draws upon a farming background as the inspiration for her work. From sheep grazing on wintry hills to farm steadings with falling-down walls and doors with rusty hinges, there is a fond familiarity in her work.

3 JANET MELROSE 01764 650 960
Has held a lifelong fascination with watercolour. Now based in Crieff, her

main inspiration comes from her surroundings and incidents that happen when she is out and about. She is particularly inspired by the vibrancy of Chinese patterns and dragons. Recent winner of the Visual Art Scotland annual show.

4 LEO DU FEU *www.leodufeu.co.uk*
Based in his home studio in Linlithgow and inspired by the natural environment. Spends much of his time exploring Scotland by bike or on foot. His paintings reflect that he is out in all weathers and captures the variety and drama of nature. Many of his works feature the Aberdeenshire coast where he has family ties. Look out for Leo's largest commission, a four-metre high depiction of land, sky and space at the Royal Observatory, Edinburgh.

5 JENNIE TUFFS
www.jennietuffs.co.uk
Best-known for vibrant flower portraits, her recent work focuses as much on exploring place and space as on natural still life. Her medium – unforgiving liquid acrylics – is deliberately chosen to reflect the need to match the subjects' own energy and light. As one of the artists commissioned by London Underground for a series of posters to brighten up the Tube, her works became familiar to many millions of Tube travellers.

86 HOTEL BARS

1 THE TULLIE INN WHLLS&T
Balloch Road, Balloch, Dunbartonshire
01389 752 052
Nestled by the banks of Loch Lomond with utterly spectacular views. The comfortable bar and lounge is ideal for soaking up the Tullie Inn atmosphere. The bar extends outside to a stunning beer garden – fully equipped for the summer with canopies, umbrellas and heating. As a hotel, The Tullie Inn is the perfect countryside retreat with 14 rooms and ideal for family holidays and cosy weekends away with that special someone.

2 ABODE GLAS/CLYDE
129 Bath Street, Glasgow 0141 572 6000
Located in the heart of the city centre and home to one of Glasgow's most stylish bars: MC Bar at ABode. Launched just over a year ago the bar has quickly established itself as one of the places to be seen with its ideal location on Bath Street. The ABode hotel itself is something of a historical landmark.

3 THE WEST PORT BAR AND KITCHEN PAD&F **South Street, St Andrews 01334 473 186**
www.thewestport.co.uk
The West Port has recently added four luxurious bedrooms to its popular St Andrews bar and restaurant which has only it made it that much more appealing. A favourite for students, the bar boasts a regular hub of evening entertainment.

4 THE HILTON GLASGOW GROSVENOR GLAS/CLYDE
1–9 Grosvenor Terrace, Glasgow 0141 337 6677
The heart of Glasgow's West End boasts one of the city's most famous and stylish drinking establishments: Bobar. Since opening last summer, Bobar has quickly established itself as one of the coolest venues Glasgow has to offer. As a hotel, the Hilton Glasgow Grosvenor offers an unrivalled location.

5 THE ABBEY INN GLAS/CLYDE
Barrhead Road, Paisley 0141 889 4529
A stylish hotel which has recently undergone a massive refurbishment to turn the downstairs lounge into a gorgeous bar diner. The Abbey is host to many an evening of entertainment as well as being the perfect place to relax, unwind and kick start your weekend. The look is fresh and bright, spacious and open and the perfect venue to enjoy a night out with friends or an intimate drink with a partner.

87 PLACES TO PROPOSE

1 OVER OYSTERS AT THE LOCH FYNE RESTAURANT WHLLS&T
Clachan, Cairndow, Argyll
01499 600 236 www.lochfyne.com
The way to a man's heart is through his stomach and he'll definitely be yours after a serving of delicious oysters at the original Loch Fyne Oyster restaurant at Cairndow. This atmospheric restaurant started life as a small shed and shop, but has grown into a thriving and truly rustic gem on the Loch Fyne shores.

2 A PERSONAL PICNIC ON THE KINNAIRD ESTATE PAD&F
Kinnaird Estate, by Dunkeld, Perthshire
01796 482 440 www.kinnairdestate.com
The rolling countryside of the luxurious Kinnaird Estate in Perthshire is simply stunning, and with a personal outdoor butler on hand to set up a romantic picnic, it's the ideal choice for creating an unforgettable proposal.

3 HYDROPOOL AT ONE SPA
EDIN/LOTH **The Sheraton Grand Hotel & Spa, 1 Festival Square, Edinburgh 0131 221 7777 www.onespa.com**
The Sheraton oozes sophistication and five-star luxury and its hydropool at One Spa is the height of relaxation. Ask the one you love to be your husband/wife while enjoying a dip in this rooftop pool. The floor-to-ceiling windows overlooking the magnificent Athens of the North, the thriving energy from the city below, coupled with the tranquillity of the hydropool is sure to get him/her hot around the collar.

4 TAKE A TANDEM RIDE WITH KATRINE WHEELZ WHLLS&T
Loch Katrine, Trossachs 01877 376 316
www.lochkatrine.com
Take your loved one on the ride of their life and propose after a thrilling tandem journey in the heart of the Trossachs with Katrine Wheelz. Cycle in unison and take in the magnificent lochside ambience, or take the bike on the morning sail boat over to Stronachlachar, where you can recreate the famous *Titanic* scene while asking the one you love to be yours forever. Bikes can be hired for one or two hours, or a half day or full day.

5 ARTHUR'S SEAT EDIN/LOTH
Holyrood Park, Edinburgh 0131 652 8150 www.historic-scotland.gov.uk
Take in the wonders of Edinburgh in the great outdoors and enjoy a romantic stroll around Arthur's Seat. Lovebirds can embark on one of the many trails around this extinct volcano and find a romantic peak to propose on as the city comes alive in the evening.

88 COUNTRY HOUSE HOTELS

1 KINNAIRD ESTATE PAD&F
near Dunkeld, Perthshire 01796 482 440
www.kinnairdestate.com
Kinnaird, perhaps the best country house hotel in Scotland, is an Edwardian mansion set in 8,000 acres of Perthshire with access to a prime salmon beat on the River Tay. It is owned and run by Connie Ward and her daughters and one of the great features is the billiard room, studded with cases of enormous stuffed salmon, mostly caught by the women of the Ward family. The food is simply wonderful, the wine list extensive and the service impeccable. Not cheap, but worth every penny.

2 DALMUNZIE PAD&F
Glenshee, Perthshire 01250 885 225
www.dalmunzie.com
Those who wearily stumble off the beaten track into this historic manor house will be delighted. Dalmunzie is a seemingly effortless combination of all the elements of countryside comfort and glamour; leather chairs by an open fire, newspapers, amiable staff and a sophisticated selection of whiskies. It is a beautiful, tranquil place.

3 DARROCH LEARG ABER/GRAMP
Braemar Road, Ballater, Aberdeenshire
01339 755 443 *www.darrochlearg.co.uk*
Perched above Ballater, the Darroch Learg has one of the most enviable views in Deeside. This becomes evident on entering, as you gaze out through one of the beautiful rooms to the glorious countryside. The three AA rosette restaurant is a must.

4 AUCHENDEAN LODGE HOTEL
HIGHLANDS **Broomhill, Dulnain Bridge**
01479 851 347 *www.auchendean.com*
This tiny converted hunting lodge may not look much, but it offers some of the best food and views anywhere in Scotland. The owners, Ian Kirk and Eric Hart, make all the meals themselves from local produce – including a breakfast with pinhead oatmeal porridge cooked slowly overnight that you will remember for years. One of Scotland's best-kept secrets.

5 EAST HAUGH HOUSE HOTEL
PAD&F **By Pitlochry, Perthshire**
01796 473 121 *www.easthaugh.co.uk*
Officially crowned 'Best Country Sports Hotel of the Year 2007' at Hotel Review Scotland.

89 COFFEE SHOPS

1 ACHILTIBUIE HYDROPONICUM
HIGHLANDS **Achiltibuie, Ullapool**
01854 622 202
www.thehydroponicum.com
A great refuge on wet west coast days when slanting rain and swirling mist make an outing to the hills an unattractive prospect. Even if your knowledge of the plant life is limited, eating fabulous cakes with a storm battering the windows outside makes for an unexpectedly enjoyable day.

2 EDZELL TWEED WAREHOUSE COFFEE SHOP PAD&F **1 Dunlappie Rd, Edzell, Angus 01356 648 675**
Attached to the Edzell Tweed Warehouse, which stocks an assortment of Scottish memorabilia including books, clothes and souvenirs. The warehouse is interesting, but you will

struggle to find soup or cakes better than those to be found in the coffee shop. The adventurous should try a slice of Tweedie special and guess the secret ingredient.

3 NORTH POINT CAFÉ PAD&F
24 North St, St Andrews 01334 473 997
Very much a student haunt, sitting opposite the university. Owes its inclusion to wonderful chocolate brownies and mugs of hot chocolate topped with whipped cream, marshmallows, chocolate buttons and Maltesers – the size options here are 'large' or 'huge'. The rest of the menu is not to be sniffed at, with the soup particularly interesting.

4 THE OLD BAKEHOUSE PAD&F
26 High Street, Brechin, Angus
The Angus town of Brechin is not well known for quality cuisine, but the Old Bakehouse is a well-kept secret. On the High Street and close to the walls of the ancient Cathedral, the paninis and other lunch items served here are filling and tasty. The homemade cake selection is excellent too.

5 SALVESEN'S COFFEE SHOP
GLAS/CLYDE **7/8 Park Terrace, Glasgow**
www.glasgowhostel.co.uk
Tucked into the basement of Glasgow Youth Hostel in the West End, Salvesen's was refurbished in 2007 and now offers a relaxing oasis in the bustling area around Kelvingrove. Light meals, hot drinks and beer and wine are served here and comfy sofas by the window are the best place to enjoy them.

90 SAILING AND FINE DINING

1 CRINAN CANAL AND CRINAN HOTEL WHLLS&T
Crinan by Lochgilphead, Argyll
01546 830 261 *www.crinanhotel.com*
What could be more glorious than sitting watching the world go by, eating freshly caught scallops and drinking cool white wine? Look around and superstars such as Rod Stewart or David Coulthard could be sitting next to you, but if you are stuck with the somewhat eccentric Crinan Hotel owner Nick Ryan, you might not leave until the wee small hours and will be in no fit state to sail anywhere. The nearby Corryvrechan Whirlpool will seem a distant thought!

2 TAYVALLICH BAY AND TAYVALLICH INN WHLLS&T
Argyll
Hidden gem that many who have been visiting over the years want to keep hidden. With a sheltered location and Gulf Stream climate, the community that thrives on sailing welcomes everyone. From the pontoon to the coffee shop, everyone is friendly, and once you have been bitten by the 'Tayvay' bug, everywhere else, with the exception of maybe Tortola in the Virgin Islands, seems boring.

3 ARDFERN WHLLS&T
Argyll
Ardfern is located near the head of Loch Craignish and is one of Scotland's most beautiful and sheltered sea lochs, which contains several islands and natural anchorages. There are about three local eateries all selling freshly caught fish and home baking. Princess

Anne keeps her boat here and as well as being a world-class marina, Ardfern Yacht Centre provides great workshop facilities.

4 CRAOBH MARINA WHLLS&T
near Lochgilphead
Formed by linking three islands together, this sheltered haven provides a central point for all that is worth exploring on the West Coast. Run by a dedicated team, it is renowned for a friendly welcome and the very best service. They have a fully enclosed workshop which can take craft in excess of 16 m for refurbishment and repair – and they offer child-friendly meals and snacks.

5 TROON YACHT HAVEN SOUTH
SCOT **Troon, Ayrshire**
If you fancy a bit more life rather than the sedate west coast havens, this is an ideal port for entering the Clyde. Accessible at all states of the tide, the marina provides a sheltered haven, nestled within the harbour of Troon and located close to the town centre where many bars and restaurants beckon.

91 GLENS

1 GLEN AFFRIC HIGHLANDS
Remote Glen Affric is one of the last bastions of Scotland's ancient Caledonian pine forest and is a stunning amalgam of natural woodland, isolated hills and windswept water. Glen Affric's depths are only accessible on foot, with the hostel and bothies, such as Strawberry Cottage, offering the best ways to discover its glories. Drive from Drumnadrochit or Beauly to the end of the A831.

2 GLEN SHIEL HIGHLANDS
Driving north-west towards Skye in half darkness (on the A87 from Loch Cluanie towards Shiel Bridge), it is impossible not to notice the sheer size of the mountains of Glen Shiel. Kintail is impressive for its sense of immensity, and driving with the south Glen Shiel ridge on one side and the Five Sisters to the north must surely strike a sense of awe into anyone travelling on the road.

3 GLEN COE HIGHLANDS
From the distinctive peak of Buachaille Etive Mor at the southern entrance to the glen, to the nail-biting edges and precipices of the Aonach Eagach ridge, to the impressive bulk of Bidean nam Bian, Glen Coe is a mountaineering dream. Ascending these summits offers the walker and climber vistas and experiences that the car-borne visitor can only imagine. In 2006, *Scotsman* readers chose Glen Coe as one of the Seven Wonders of Scotland – it was championed by Sir Jimmy Savile, who has a house there. Get there on the A82 north, just before you get to Ballachulish.

4 GLEN BRITTLE HIGHLANDS
Glenbrittle is the access point to arguably the finest mountaineering ridge in the British Isles, the Black Cuillin of Skye. The ridge is breathtakingly lovely in sunshine but can have an other-worldly severity when the clouds descend and the mountains are wrapped in rain and mist. The safety of Glen Brittle is often reached with an air of relief. Come off the A863 onto the B8009 and head south on a minor road off to your left.

5 GLENFESHIE HIGHLANDS
The Cairngorm plateau boasts a

plethora of stunning and remote inland glens. Lovely Glenfeshie skirts the edge of the central plateau and gives access to some less-frequently visited hills, notably Sgorr Gaoith, the 'Peak of the Wind'. The summit is perched precipitously on cliffs that fall steeply away to Loch Einich far below and the view towards Ben MacDui is one of the best in the Cairngorms. Leave the A9 for the B970 and head south from Feshiebridge.

92 SEALIFE CENTRES

1 LOCH LOMOND AQUARIUM

WHLLS&T Loch Lomond Shores, Balloch 01389 721 500 www.sealifeeurope.com
There's absolutely no doubt who are the stars of the show at this sealife centre – Shona, Mona and Rhona, who probably have their own dressing room somewhere. These Asiatic otters make high-pitched squeals, jump around, wrestle and generally play up to an audience who are held in rapture. Although the other displays are excellent, the gilled entertainment seems decidedly boring in comparison.

2 DEEP SEA WORLD EDIN/LOTH

Battery Quarry, North Queensferry, Fife 01383 411 880 www.deepseaworld.com
The 112 m long underwater tunnel is the most impressive exhibit at this centre. Creep along while sand tiger sharks and giant rays glide sinisterly over your head. The slight frisson of fear continues with a display of piranhas and a Krakatoa tank full of creatures dying to nibble or poison you. Kids aged eight to 15 can get involved in diving on a 45-minute Bubblemaker course in the giant tanks.

3 THE SCOTTISH SEABIRD CENTRE

EDIN/LOTH The Harbour, North Berwick, East Lothian 01620 890 202
www.seabird.org
The entrance fee to this seabird centre is quite high, considering the exhibits are generally rather lame for people over knee height. There is one saving grace: you can manipulate specially-positioned cameras to view live streaming of gulls and puffins nesting on nearby cliffs and gannets on Bass Rock.

4 THE SCOTTISH SEALIFE

SANCTUARY WHLLS&T Barcaldine, Oban, Argyll 01631 720 386
www.sealsanctuary.co.uk
This place, beside the picturesque Loch Crenan, is primarily a rescue centre for seals but still offers an opportunity for us to gawp at fish in tanks. Aside from the resident shrimp, stingray and sharks in their aquarium with its distinct Pirates of the Caribbean theme, they have also got a few other mammalian stars at their otter sanctuary, which houses a couple of native European otters.

5 ST ANDREWS AQUARIUM PAD&F

The Scores, St Andrews, Fife 01334 474 786
www.standrewsaquarium.co.uk
The pair of seals, Laurel and Hardy, are the big draw here: don't miss feeding time. There are also another 30 tanks full of oddities, including the spiny porcupine fish, wolf-fish and a shoal of piranhas.

93 SCOTS WORDS

1 BAUCHLE

Originally used to refer to a wee, fat,

untidy wifie. When the whole heroin chic thing was in, girls would have taken it as a compliment to be called a 'bauchle', but now with a return to the Jackie O school of wardrobe a modern-day usage might be 'that Kate Moss might be a malinky size zero, but in that mockit simmit she still looks a right bauchle'.

2 BLETHER
A classic and favourite – a friendly word to mean idle chitter chatter. May have been used to describe women as they swapped gossip at the steamie, but is now used to refer to all sorts of situations involving women and what we do best: 'Let's go to Harvey Nichols and have a good old blether over some champagne cocktails.'

3 DREICH
Used to describe grey, damp, nondescript days, the kind that in the school holidays when you were young inevitably meant a trip to a museum or other such place where learning was supposed to be fun.

4 FANKLE
Applied to wool that becomes tangled up, but can now be used to mean any sort of muddle, such as: 'Oh, the earphones for my brand new 40GB iPod Nano are in a proper fankle.'

5 GALLUS
Bold, daring, rash, wild, unmanageable, impish, mischievous, cheeky. Usage: 'Yi gallus wee besom, I'll skelp yir erse!'. Translation: 'Ooh, you are a one, I'll put you over my knee!'

6 MOOCH
Slightly confusing in its exact definition. The west seems to use it to mean to

scrounge/acquire through blagging, while in the east it seems to mean to be nosey, inquisitive.

7 POCHLE
To describe a thief or the act of thieving. Almost an affectionate term though: 'Oi, who's pochled my stapler?' or 'Don't leave that there, you're just inviting someone to pochle it'.

8 SLITTER
Can be used to refer to a spillage of something, but also a complicated situation. Modern use might be: 'Oh golly, I've slittered spaghetti all down my new retro 'Frankie says' T-shirt.'

9 WABBIT
Just such an excellent way to describe the feeling the morning after the night before, a slight chill and general run-down feeling at the onslaught of a cold, or simply how you might feel after a long day at work – tired, worn out, peely-wally.

10 WHEESHT
A dismissive expression to encourage someone to be quiet: 'Haud yer wheesht ye sooth-moothed eejit, ye dinnae ken what yer havering aboot.' Translation: 'Do hush up chap from anywhere south of Lerwick, I'm not sure you truly grasp the concept that's being discussed.'

94 PLACES TO SEE THE RED DEER RUT

Each autumn, the mountains and hillsides are the venue for the rut of the red deer stag. Roars and bellows echo from the rutting grounds in the quest

BLETHER

DREICH

WHEESHT

to establish male hierarchy and determine breeding rights. When two stags are evenly matched, a fight ensues. The locking of antlers is violent and dangerous: each year, about five per cent of the stags are permanently injured.

1 GALLOWAY FOREST PARK
SOUTH SCOT 01671 402 420
www.forestry.gov.uk
From the Red Deer Range car park (off the A712), a half-mile way-marked trail leads you to a viewing area where you can see red deer in a semi-natural habitat. There are ranger-led guided walks throughout the year.

2 HIGHLAND ADVENTURE SAFARIS
PAD&F Drumdewan, Aberfeldy
01887 820 071
www.highlandadventuresafaris.co.uk
At this time of year, it is perhaps not advisable to get too close to Scotland's largest land animal: the testosterone in the bloodstream makes stags highly unpredictable. For this reason, the safest and most reliable way to get close to the action is on a Roaring Stag Safari from Highland Adventure Safaris.

3 HIGHLAND WILDLIFE PARK
HIGHLANDS Kingussie 01540 651 270
www.highlandwildlifepark.org
The red deer herd in the park's main reserve exhibit the dynamics of a truly wild herd and, as such, the behaviour of the stags each autumn is no different to those true monarchs of the glen.
So, from the safety and relative comfort of your car, you can experience this most impressive wildlife spectacle.

4 RUM NATIONAL NATURE RESERVE HIGHLANDS 01687 462 026
www.nnr-scotland.org.uk

Rum, the largest of the Small Isles, is quite simply 'red deer island'. The deer are one of the most intensively studied large mammal populations in the world. Scientists have carried out research on them for 50 years.

5 SCOTTISH DEER CENTRE PAD&F
Cupar, Fife 01337 810 391
www.ewm.co.uk/tourist-shops-visitor-centres/scottish-deer-centre.htm
As well as red deer, the centre has eight other species of deer. After walking round the 55-acre park on a cold October day, the Courtyard Coffee Shop's soup and home baking are a godsend.

95 JAZZ VENUES

1 JAZZ AT HOSPITALFIELD PAD&F
West Way, Arbroath 01382 774 648
www.hospitalfield.org.uk
Now in its 18th year, this is one of Scotland's best-known venues, set in the impressive surroundings of historic Hospitalfield House. Concerts are held monthly and feature both UK and international artists covering most styles of jazz and blues. The venue holds 120 – seated at small tables – and there is a bar.

2 JAZZ AT THE LOT EDIN/LOTH
4–6 Grassmarket, Edinburgh
0131 225 9924 *www.the-lot.co.uk*
Located at the corner of the Grassmarket and Kings Stables Road, this is Edinburgh's top jazz venue. This converted church has a light and airy feel and seating is at small tables. There is a bistro and bar. Local, national and international acts appear at the Lot throughout the year on most nights of the week.

3 THE LYTH ARTS CENTRE

HIGHLANDS **Lyth, Wick, Caithness**
01955 641 270 *www.lytharts.org.uk*
Situated deep in the Caithness
countryside, this is the most northerly
mainland jazz venue. From the outside,
the building has retained the character
of a Victorian country school but,
inside, it has been converted to a
dynamic multi-purpose arts centre.

4 THE OLD COURSE HOTEL PAD&F

Old Station Road, St Andrews, Fife
01334 474 371
www.oldcoursehotel.co.uk
The emphasis is on mellow acoustic
music, featuring mainly Scottish
musicians with the occasional guest
artist. Admission is free. There is a bar
and delicious savoury and sweet crêpes
can be purchased.

5 LINLITHGOW JAZZ CLUB

EDIN/LOTH **Burg Halls, High Street,**
Linlithgow, West Lothian 01506 848 821
www.linlithgowjazzclub.co.uk
This well-established club is held in the
Burgh Halls in Linlithgow. The music
veers towards the traditional end of the
jazz scale, from either guest bands or
the resident West End Jazz Band.
Concerts are held two or three times
per month throughout the year.

96 PIZZAS

1 HEAVENLY PIZZAS EDIN/LOTH

18 Home Street, Tollcross, Edinburgh
0131 228 6656
www.heavenlypizzas.com
Produces fun and exciting new pizzas
unique to the company, including The
Heavenly Breakfast Special – the perfect
hangover cure. No need to leave the
comfort of your own home either, with

a full licence to deliver beer and wine, a
fairly unusual, but heavenly service has
arrived.

2 JOLLY'S EDIN/LOTH

9 Elm Row, Edinburgh 0131 556 1588
Uses a proper wood-fired pizza oven so
there are no horrible spongy pizza
bases. They're cheap too (about £7 for a
pizza that will feed two quite greedy
people) and they deliver to your door
within 15 minutes of ordering.

3 PRIMA PIZZA EDIN/LOTH

8 Polwarth Gardens, Edinburgh
0131 228 3090
Under new management, this has
become Edinburgh's hidden gem.
Dough is fresh every day, so the bases
are as good as bread you find in a
baker and the tomato sauce is fresh and
juicy. The menu has improved in
standard and quality and the chef will
make you any pizza you order, or even
suggest some tasty options of his own
up to a whopping 16in. Great.

4 BELLA ITALIA EDIN/LOTH

12 High Street, North Berwick
01620 893 916
The calzone – mushrooms, ham and
chicken, with the pizza folded over and
sealed to take on the shape of a rugby
ball – in magnificent. Celebrated its
25th anniversary in 2006 and the food is
the same high quality as ever.

5 CAFFE LUCANO EDIN/LOTH

37–39 George IV Bridge, Edinburgh
0131 225 6690
If you like your pizza thin and crispy
with fresh, top-quality, traditional
ingredients – think anchovies, olives,
pepperoni – then this is the place for
you. Good cakes and coffee for afters.

97 MUSEUMS

1 NATIONAL MUSEUM OF SCOTLAND EDIN/LOTH
Chambers Street, Edinburgh
0131 247 4422 *www.nms.ac.uk*
Starting below ground level, the visitor is introduced to the geological origins of Scotland, and then prehistoric men and women start their role of bringing agriculture to the countryside.
Although not the first settlers, the Romans and their arms and monuments play an important part in this level of the museum. Moving up through the floors takes you through the various ages of history, on to the industrial revolution, the many emigrations to the new world and eventually into modern times. Well worth a visit – or two, or three. Promises to get even better after the big refurb.

2 THE PEOPLE'S PALACE GLAS/CLYDE
Glasgow Green, Glasgow
0141 271 2962
www.glasgowmuseums.com
Set in the middle of Glasgow Green, this museum charts the development of the history of trade unionism and the labour movement, highlighting many of the protests that have dominated Scottish history. Great use of oral history and old cinema footage. Puts the modern day into perspective.

3 ABERDEEN MARITIME MUSEUM
ABER/GRAMP **52–56 Shiprow, Aberdeen**
01224 337 700 *www.aagm.co.uk*
This museum plays an important role in telling the story of how the seas around Scotland's shores have helped mould its history, civilisation and culture. Not just about boats, it also helps to show how North Sea oil and gas helped

dramatically change the destiny of all of Scotland – and particularly the North East.

4 DISCOVERY POINT ANTARCTIC MUSEUM PAD&F **Discovery Point, Dundee 01382 201 245**
www.rrsdiscovery.com
An excellent visitor and interpretive centre for the *Discovery* vessel now permanently sited conveniently close to the centre of Dundee and its railway station. A great way to find out why this beautiful city by the Tay is described as the City of Discovery. Watch out for the exhibition's excellent finale, in which modern-day film and technology brings the ship to life.

5 INVERNESS MUSEUM HIGHLANDS
Castle Wynd, Inverness 01463 237 114
www.invernessmuseum.com
Conveniently located at the start of the Great Glen Way and provides an excellent introduction to the history of the Highlands. Puts Nessie in perspective.

98 FERRY JOURNEYS

1 GLENELG TO KYLERHEA
HIGHLANDS **01599 522 273** *or* **522 313**
www.skyeferry.co.uk
This is a spectacular crossing that doesn't take much more than five minutes. The drive alone is a good enough excuse to get here. Turn left at Shiel Bridge and follow the single-track road from the sea, up and over the summit of Mam Ratagan before descending back to sea level at Glenelg. In ancient times, the cattle drovers used to swim their cattle from Kylerhea, on Skye, to Glenelg, on the mainland, before taking them south to sell. The

crossing is a distance of less than 600 m. Dolphins, porpoises, otters and eagles may all be spotted.

2 STORNOWAY TO ULLAPOOL
OUT. ISLES – HIGHLANDS
booking hotline 08000 665 000
www.calmac.co.uk
Sit back, relax and admire the coastline of the north-west Highlands as you cross the Minch from Stornoway to Ullapool. Great views ranging from Cape Wrath in the north-west to the mountains of Torridon in the south. Switching your gaze away from the mainland you can also admire the majesty of the Isle of Skye, which is visible to the south most of the way across. If your luck is in, then you stand a good chance of seeing dolphins, porpoises and occasionally whales. Crossing takes just over two and a half hours.

3 SCRABSTER TO STROMNESS
HIGHLANDS – OUT. ISLES
www.northlinkferries.co.uk
Another crossing offering superb views. Given good weather you should be able to view the whole north coast, from Cape Wrath in the far north-west to Duncansby Head in the north-east. Even more dramatic is the view of the Old Man of Hoy, rising vertically some 140 m out of the sea. The crossing to Orkney takes about 90 minutes.

4 BARRA TO OBAN OUT. ISLES –
WHLLS&T **08000 665 000**
www.calmac.co.uk
This crossing takes about five hours: plenty time to enjoy a dram or two while admiring the scenery. Leaving Castlebay, you pass Kisimul Castle, the ancestral home of the McNeil clan and head east towards the distant

mainland. Ardnamurchan Point, the most westerly place on mainland Britain, will be visible, as will the mountains of Mull. As you approach the Sound of Mull, you leave the open Atlantic behind.

5 FIONNPHORT TO IONA, WHLLS&T
08000 665 000 *www.calmac.co.uk*
A 10 minute crossing takes you from the Isle of Mull to Iona, the birthplace of Christianity in Scotland. By going to Iona, you are also following in the path of the ancient kings of Scotland. Iona was their final destination. It was here that they were buried.

99 CATHEDRALS

1 ST MAGNUS CATHEDRAL OUT.
ISLES **Broad Street, Kirkwall, Orkney 01856 874 894** *www.orkney.gov.uk*
The magnificent red sandstone of St Magnus Cathedral dominates the centre of Kirkwall, the Orcadian capital. The mediaeval structure – the most northerly cathedral in the British Isles – was given to the people of Kirkwall by James III when the Orkney Isles became part of Scotland. Today, it is used as a Church of Scotland parish church and also for concerts. As well as touring the fascinating interior of the cathedral, the nearby Bishop's and Earl's palaces are also worth a visit.

2 DUNBLANE CATHEDRAL PAD&F
The Cross, Dunblane, Perthshire 01786 825 388
www.dunblanecathedral.org.uk
Like many cathedrals, the interior of Dunblane is calm and meditative. The beautiful building, the base to a large Church of Scotland congregation, also contains a memorial to those killed

at the local primary school in the Dunblane tragedy. There is also a pleasant walk along the river.

3 ST GILES' CATHEDRAL EDIN/LOTH
Royal Mile, Edinburgh 0131 225 9442
www.stgilescathedral.org.uk
Sitting at the very heart of the Scottish capital, St Giles' Cathedral, sometimes called the High Kirk of Edinburgh, has a central role in the civic life of the nation. It's from inside the church's tall stone walls that the parliament is 'kirked', new knights are admitted to the Order of the Thistle and many large funerals take place.

4 ST ANDREWS CATHEDRAL PAD&F
St Andrews, Fife 01334 472 563
www.historic-scotland.gov.uk
This ruin of one of Scotland's most famous cathedrals is a place of wonder. Attacked at the very start of the Reformation in 1559, the cathedral slowly fell into disrepair and its stone was quarried for building work in the town. The stones in the graveyard are also fascinating.

5 ST MARY'S CHURCH EDIN/LOTH
Haddington, East Lothian
www.stmaryskirk.com
Perhaps not a true cathedral but St Mary's Parish Church in Haddington – the 'Lamp of Lothian' – is worth a visit. The full church building was brought back to life in the early 1970s in a remarkable restoration project.

100 FISHING VILLAGES

1 CROVIE ABER/GRAMP
(Between Banff and Fraserburgh)
Aberdeenshire

The ideal fishing village. Established in the late 18th century to provide homes for inland families supplanted by sheep. Around 40 beautifully-maintained cottages hunker below precipitous cliffs. There's no vehicular access: the causeway between houses and sea is just too narrow. Residents park at the village-end and use barrows.

2 GARDENSTOWN ABER/GRAMP
(Between Banff and Fraserburgh)
Aberdeenshire
Across Gamrie Bay from Crovie, this large village has a fishertoun at sea level with old cottages gable-end to the sea. Newer houses and chapels rise in steep terraces above the harbour. Gardenstown is the site of British Gnome Stores' flagship shed.

3 CELLARDYKE PAD&F
Anstruther, Fife
The eastern extension of Anstruther. The long main street has been conserved but not over-prettified. Here you can stand, magic away the cars, and picture the bustle and busyness of herring-boom days. Can it be true that the name is a corruption of sil'erdykes, referring to the shine of herring scales in nets hanging over walls to dry in the sun? More recently, the village was at the centre of a national bird flu scare, when a dead swan washed up.

4 SANDEND ABER/GRAMP
(Between Banff and Buckie) **Moray**
Three miles from Portsoy, this is one of the smallest and best of the Moray coast fishing villages. Close-packed houses, some particularly distinctive with the multi-coloured stones of their walls outlined in white, then painted black with an irregular patch left bare.

Beach popular with families and surfers overlooked by well-preserved set of Second World War anti-tank blocks like the teeth of a stranded and sand-buried leviathan. Sandend also has a campsite by the beach.

5 FITTIE ABER/GRAMP
Aberdeen
The popular name, Fittie, long predates, and is not a corruption of the official designation, Footdee. Early 19th century squares with windowless house-backs facing outwards. Sited at the entrance to Aberdeen Harbour and overlooked by the new, lighthouse-inspired maritime operations centre. Inside and around the squares there are old tarry sheds, maritime bric-a-brac, washing lines, flowers and vegetables. Some of its other features include navigation lamps, which are used to light the low doorways and ships in bottles sitting in the windows.

101 OUTDOOR ACTIVITY OPERATORS

1 PUFFIN DIVE CENTRE WHLLS&T
Port Gallanach, by Oban 01631 566 088
www.puffin.org.uk
Some would bat more than an eyelid at the prospect of diving in the dark and chilly waters off the west coast of Scotland but this is exactly what you are encouraged to do at arguably Scotland's best dive centre. 'Try a Dive' sessions are offered for beginners and regular boat trips take seasoned divers to wrecks and other sites.

2 ROCKHOPPER SEA KAYAKING
HIGHLANDS **Corpach, by Fort William**

www.rockhopperscotland.co.uk
Sea kayaking is one of the finest ways to explore Scotland's intricate west coast and Rockhopper Sea Kayaking offers guided trips and instruction in a range of locations to help you do just that. A great way to see Loch Leven from a different perspective or watch seals and otters around tiny coastal islands by Arisaig.

3 ARRAN ADVENTURE COMPANY
SOUTH SCOT **Brodick 01770 302 244**
www.arranadventure.com
Arran is often described as Scotland in miniature and the Arran Adventure Company offers a range of the best adventure activities that Scotland has to offer: abseiling, climbing, mountain biking, gorge walking, canyoning, sea kayaking and archery.

4 CAPE ADVENTURE INTERNATIONAL HIGHLANDS
by Lairg 01971 521 006
www.capeventure.co.uk
Based in the wild and isolated northern Highlands, the Cape Adventure outdoor centre offers an excellent range of activities for adults, young people or families, including walking, sea kayaking, climbing, orienteering, surfing and land yachting.

5 NAE LIMITS PAD&F
by Dunkeld 08450 178 177
www.naelimits.co.uk
Nae Limits, near Perth, is one of Scotland's best centres for high-adrenaline activities. White-water rafting, canyoning and cliff jumping are the order of the day here. Nae Limits also remains the only Scottish outdoor activity centre to offer 'sphering' – rolling downhill in a giant rubber ball.

102 ALL-DAY WALKS

1 COVE TO BRIDGE OF DON

ABER/GRAMP **Aberdeen** *(11 miles)*
Starts with a three-mile cliff walk along spectacular coastline, then takes in Nigg Bay, Girdleness Lighthouse, panoramic views of the port and sea front, dolphin-spotting, the Dee estuary, maritime museum, harbour bustling with large and colourful oil-support vessels, funfair, pleasure beach, traditional cafés, long promenade marked by red footprints, Don estuary and nature reserve.

2 PORTSOY TO FINDOCHTY

ABER/GRAMP **Moray Coast** *(12 miles)*
Begins at Portsoy's restored Medieval harbour and takes in old fishing villages, picturesque harbours, beaches, cliffs, viewpoints and headlands. The Whale's Mouth and Fiddler's Bow rocks near Portknockie are appropriately named, as is the amazing Giant's Steps. Cullen is the place to queue for ice-cream and to sample a bowl of Cullen Skink. Walk finishes in the pronunciation-challenging Findochty ('Finnechty').

3 BERWICK-ON-TWEED TO ST ABB'S

SOUTH SCOT *(14 miles)*
Three miles beyond the bridges, beaches and fortifications of Berwick and you're clambering over a stile into Scotland. You'll see cliffs, clefts, wave-sculpted sandstone, teeming and screaming seabirds, rock-pool shores, glaucous leaves of salt-sprinkled plants, Eyemouth harbour and Coldingham beach.

4 LOWER LARGO TO CRAIL PAD&F

Fife Coastal Path *(12 miles)*

Low-level walk from the birthplace of Alexander Selkirk, the model for Robinson Crusoe, to one of the most painted scenes in Scotland, the view over Crail harbour. Then it's on to the chocolate-box-top East Neuk villages of St Monans and Pittenweem. Anstruther is a mecca for fish-and-chip lovers.

5 PORTOBELLO TO ABERLADY

EDIN/LOTH *(13 miles)*
Enjoy the day-tripper delights of Portobello, the swan-flecked Esk estuary, Levenhall Links reclaimed from the sea using ash from Cockenzie power station, Prestongrange Industrial Heritage Museum, big ships in the Forth, assorted wading birds darting and dipping throughout and the sandy sea-flats of Aberlady Local Nature Reserve.

103 SEABIRD-WATCHING

1 ST ABB'S HEAD SOUTH SCOT

Berwickshire
One of the most readily accessible seabird colonies. Formed by active volcanoes, St Abb's Head is the best-known landmark along this magnificent coastline. Here, a complex coastline of sheer cliffs, offshore stacks and narrow gullies provides scenic beauty and a habitat for some outstanding wildlife. Although best known as a seabird colony, this National Nature Reserve includes 200 acres of grasslands rich in flowers, a freshwater loch and a steady stream of migrant birds in spring and autumn. Get there from the A1 by following the A1107 to the Berwick-shire Coastal Trail. At Coldingham, take the B6438 to St Abb's, then follow signs for the Nature Reserve.

2 ISLE OF MAY EDIN/LOTH
Firth of Forth

Five miles south-east of the Fife villages of Anstruther and Crail and just over a mile long, the Isle of May is a haven for thousands of nesting seabirds and supports a large grey seal colony. It has been a National Nature Reserve since 1956. The western cliffs rise to nearly 150 ft and are home to some 20,000 pairs of guillemots, 7,000 kittiwakes and 2,000 razorbills, with hundreds of pairs of fulmars and shags. However, the puffin is the real star of the May in summer. Over the past 50 years, numbers have risen to as many as 70,000 pairs. The *May Princess* sails from Anstruther – 01333 310 103 or visit www.isleofmayferry.com – and *Aquatrek* sails on Wednesdays and Thursdays from North Berwick. Tel: 07790 929 656 or visit www.aquatrek.co.uk

3 FOWLSHEUGH ABER/GRAMP
near Stonehaven

Just south of the spectacular Dunnottar Castle near Stonehaven, the sheer cliffs of the RSPB's Fowlsheugh Reserve stretch for three miles, standing high over the North Sea. The cliffs hold thousands of boulder-shaped hollows. Over 80,000 seabirds nest here, truly one of nature's spectacles. The most abundant resident is the guillemot, with 50,000 nesting birds. Other common species are the kittiwake (10,000 pairs) and razorbill (4,000 birds), similar to the guillemot. There are puffins here too. On the rocks below, grey and common seals can be seen, while out to sea there are bottle-nosed and white-beaked dolphins, along with occasional minke whales. Stonehaven

lies on the railway, with frequent services. Hourly bus services run from Stonehaven, stopping at the Crawton turn-off (one mile walk to the reserve). By car, take the Crawton turn from the A92 Stonehaven to Inverbervie road and park in the car park by the cliffs near Crawton.

4 SUMBURGH HEAD OUT. ISLES
Shetland

This easily recognisable headland is home to thousands of breeding seabirds. It is one of the most accessible seabird colonies in Britain, with puffins, guillemots, kittiwakes, fulmars, shags and razorbills easily viewed in safety. The coastal grassland is also important for breeding wheatears, twite and Shetland wrens and starlings. With commanding views over the North Sea and Atlantic Ocean, it is a prime location for spotting everything from porpoises to humpback whales. Minke whales and orca are frequent summer visitors.

5 NOUP CLIFFS OUT. ISLES
Westray, Orkney

Lying at the north-western extremity of the Orkney Isles, this is one of the most spectacular bird experiences in Scotland. The Devonian Old Red Sandstone has here been weathered into horizontal ledges that provide ideal nesting sites for tens of thousands of seabirds, the sheer cliffs facing west into the Atlantic with no land between here and southern Greenland. The colony extends along almost the whole five-mile stretch of the west coast of Westray, but it is the northernmost 1.5 mile section that holds the highest densities of birds. Counts last summer revealed Noup Cliffs still hold over 50,000 guillemots, 800 razorbills, 12,000 pairs of kittiwakes and 600 pairs of fulmars, and smaller numbers of shags, puffins and black guillemots.

More info: www.rspb.org.uk/scotland/

104 BIKE RIDES

1 UNION CANAL, FORTH AND CLYDE CANAL EDIN/LOTH – GLAS/CLYDE Edinburgh to Glasgow
www.scottishcanals.co.uk
The 58-mile path along the Union Canal and the Forth and Clyde Canal is the best. It's your very own cycling superhighway, linking Glasgow and Edinburgh, with just a detour through Falkirk, where the waterways meet.

2 ISLE OF CUMBRAE SOUTH SCOT
www.millport.org
Take the ferry to Cumbrae and cycle round the coast. It's a 10 mile ride around the edge, but you can also take some central paths. You can take your bike on the ferry or you can hire one at Millport.

3 INVERNESS TO DOCHGARROCH
HIGHLANDS *www.scottishcanals.co.uk*
Start at Tomnahurich Bridge on the A82 in Inverness and head for Dochgarroch, along the Caledonian Canal. It follows the canal towpath for about four miles and is flat, so no pesky hills – and good for kids too. Watch the boats going up and down the canal and view the River Ness on the other side. Once at Dochgarroch, you can picnic by the canal, watching the boats negotiate the locks, or make use of the tea shop, which sells good ice-cream.

4 KIRKLISTON TO SOUTH QUEENSFERRY EDIN/LOTH
Ideal return trip for a family because almost all of its length is easy and traffic-free. There is a short section near Dalmeny where an eroded set of steps must be negotiated, but apart from this, it's plain sailing. From Kirkliston, the path runs through a tunnel of trees. At Dalmeny it parallels the main railway line before sweeping under the impressive arches of the Forth Bridge. There are splendid views of the Firth of Forth and Fife.

5 THE INNOCENT RAILWAY
EDIN/LOTH Edinburgh to Musselburgh
Most of this route follows the Innocent Railway Line, which has been converted into a well-surfaced path with easy gradients. Within five minutes of cycling along the path, the hustle and bustle of Edinburgh is left behind – the route offers spectacular views of Arthur's Seat, passes through fields and ends by the sea.

105 CHINESE FOOD

1 CATHAY CUISINE EDIN/LOTH
25 Main Street, Deans, Livingston
01506 409 988
Restaurants and takeaways too often rely only on the common dishes which will be fine for most people, but what if you have a more eclectic taste and fancy a change from the usual? Cathay Cuisine does all the favourites, but also offers some brilliant, more unusual plates such as Five-spice Chicken. It is a taste explosion, bursting full of flavour and it doesn't come swimming in a vat of sauce.

2 THE UNICORN EDIN/LOTH
112 St Stephen's Street, Edinburgh
0131 220 4799
With specials on a whiteboard and rice

served at the table in Tupperware boxes, this isn't one of the most sophisticated restaurants, but it is a hidden gem. Busy every day of the week and often visited by Edinburgh's Chinese community, the food is fresh, tasty and without any of that every-dish-the-same problem that often befalls Chinese restaurants. Service is always friendly and welcoming.

3 CHOW GLAS/CLYDE
98 Byres Road, Glasgow 0141 334 9818
Head and shoulders above its competitors, Chow has a great menu with lots of healthier options than the majority of Chinese takeaways. Their noodle dishes are particularly delicious.

4 PEKING PALACE GLAS/CLYDE
East Kilbride Road, Rutherglen, Glasgow 0141 634 2998
Proving that good service can be priority even with takeaway food, the Peking Palace in the Royal Burgh of Rutherglen keeps customers coming back for more by ensuring that their takeaway orders are of the same quality as the food served up in the main restaurant. This is not a place for modern, innovative, fusion Asian cuisine, but you will find all the family favourites – such as sweet and sour chicken and Peking duck – in generous portions and accompanied with the restaurant's famous prawn crackers. A delicious, decadent trip down memory lane.

5 CHOP CHOP EDIN/LOTH
248 Morrison Street, Edinburgh 0131 221 1155
A very different Chinese, with dozens and dozens of different dumplings, all of which are delicious. The main courses

are also very varied and often unusual and the real selling-point is that it is very busy and hard to get a big table. Great for a group night out.

6 THE HONG CHINESE RESTAURANT
EDIN/LOTH **149 Uphall Station Road, Pumpherston 01506 441 832**
www.hong-restaurant.co.uk
An 'all-you-can-eat' buffet with a difference – instead of the food lying in heated containers from which you serve yourself, they serve you the starters and/or appetisers. They then take your order for your choice(s) of the main courses. They are then cooked and served fresh to you. Any further choices are cooked when required. Steadily increasing the customer base through the quality and quantity of their food and excellent service.

106 WAR MEMORIALS

1 BIRSE WAR MEMORIAL
ABER/GRAMP **Finzean, Aberdeenshire**
Finzean war memorial is most striking when driving east along the South Deeside Road. Just past the village of Finzean, the road rises to the summit of Corsedardar hill and the sight of the granite memorial, set against the backdrop of the Grampian mountains and the distinctive rocky tor on Clachnaben. Surely a fitting reminder of the sacrifices made by so many.

2 EDZELL WAR MEMORIAL PAD&F
Edzell, Angus
The striking grey needle in the Angus village of Edzell lies on the wide and attractive High Street amid beautifully kept gardens. 'We owe more tears to

these dead men than time shall see us pay,' reads the inscription , which is undoubtedly treated with the respect that those for whom it was erected deserve.

3 TOBERMORY WAR MEMORIAL
WHLLS&T **Isle of Mull**
The memorial in Tobermory is at the top of the hill above the town. Although the spire is striking in itself, the view from the hilltop, taking in Tobermory harbour and the Sound of Mull, lends it a divine majesty that pulls at the heartstrings.

4 ST ANDREWS WAR MEMORIAL
PAD&F **St Andrews, Fife**
The distinguished war memorial in Scotland's ancient religious capital lies at the end of North Street, between the attractive stone university buildings and the ruined cathedral. It is somehow a fitting location for a memorial in a town so marked by the effects of learning and war.

5 BARRA WAR MEMORIAL
OUT. ISLES **Barra**
Sited on the road to Vatersay at the crest of the hill overlooking Castlebay and the islands to the south of Barra, this memorial is strikingly modern, erected in 1993. It was raised to rectify the omission of the names of the men of Barra from a stained glass memorial window in the church of Our Lady Star of the Sea, in Castlebay.

107 PLACES TO SEE RED SQUIRRELS

1 BRODICK CASTLE AND COUNTRY PARK SOUTH SCOT **Arran,** *Grid Ref NS*
015375, **01770 302 462** *www.nts.org.uk*
There are 10 miles of woodland trails in the grounds of Brodick Castle, with spectacular views across Brodick Bay and the Ayrshire coast. Guided walks are available, which offer a straightforward way to see red squirrels.

2 DRUMLANRIG CASTLE AND COUNTRY PARK SOUTH SCOT
Dumfriesshire *Grid Ref NX 846985,* **01848 331 555** *www.drumlanrig.com*
The visitor centre relays live images of red squirrels from feeding stations in the woods. However, visitors are encouraged to explore almost 80 miles of trails to observe red squirrels for themselves.

3 GLENMORE FOREST PARK VISITOR CENTRE HIGHLANDS
Inverness-shire, *Grid Ref NH 978098* **01479 861 220** *www.forestry.gov.uk*
This ancient habitat is ideal for red squirrels, and visitors are more than likely to observe them from the café in the visitor centre.

4 GIGHT WOOD WILDLIFE RESERVE
ABER/GRAMP **Aberdeenshire,** *Grid Ref NJ 820392* **0131 312 7765** *www.swt.org.uk*
The most natural of these five locations, Gight Wood does not have a visitor centre or amenities. However, rope bridges in the wood enable the squirrels to cross the River Ythan to exploit a particularly rich source of hazelnuts.

5 LOCH OF THE LOWES VISITOR CENTRE PAD&F **Perthshire,** *Grid Ref NO 050440* **01350 727 337** *www.swt.org.uk*

For many, the main draw of Loch of the Lowes Wildlife Reserve is the return of breeding osprey each April. However, bird feeders produce an unforgettable experience when red squirrels descend.

108 ALTERNATIVE TOURIST ATTRACTIONS

1 THE ITALIAN CHAPEL OUT. ISLES
South Ronaldsay, Orkney
An Italian PoW Nissen hut from the Second World War made into a beautiful chapel from such raw materials as driftwood and corned beef tins. After visiting the chapel, check out the Churchill barriers and blockships on the A961, protecting Scapa Flow to this day. A second attraction close to the Italian Chapel is the Tomb of the Eagles. Thousands of years old, this is a private neolithic site on South Ronaldsay where you have to lie on a skateboard to get inside. The small but fascinating museum has a great many skulls and other artefacts.

2 THE PINEAPPLE WHLLS&T
Airth
Signposted off the A905 Stirling-Grangemouth road. What can you say? It's a very big stone pineapple.
The Pineapple can actually be rented out for holidaymakers. Imagine the postcard with the line 'I've rented a Pineapple'. Unmissable, even if all you do is go and look.

3 BEN CRUACHAN WHLLS&T
(A85, midway between Tyndrum and Oban)
A chance to take an electric bus – what else, it's a power station – right inside a mountain to see the hydro power plant. Plus, it's always about 17°C no matter when you go.

4 ELECTRIC BRAE SOUTH SCOT
Ayrshire
On the A719 between Dunure and Croy Bay. Release handbrake and watch the car roll uphill. Who cares if it's an optical illusion?

5 STATUE TO COLONEL STIRLING
WHLLS&T *(founder of the SAS, on the B824)*
On the 'back road' between Stirling/Dunblane and Doune on the B824. A stylish and striking monument to a brave man. It has to be said that this puts the Mel Gibson/*Braveheart* statue at the National Wallace Monument to shame. This one has a bit of class.

6 CRINAN CANAL WHLLS&T
Argyll, 01546 603 210 *(lock inquiries)*
www.scottishcanals.co.uk
Not a museum but living history. Built with the help of Thomas Telford, you can still view the sometimes quirky bridges and locks. Walk its length on a sunny summer's day on the towpath or just sit and watch the boats glide silently by.

7 FERGUSSON GALLERY PAD&F
Marshall Place, Perth 01738 441 944
www.pkc.gov.uk
Among the stiff competition of galleries in Scotland, this wins out as it shows mainly the work of J.D. Fergusson, the Scottish colourist, and as a result shows it in some depth. Marvel at the paintings as well as the building – a rescued and renovated circular water tower situated next to the beautiful Tay near the town centre.

8 MUSEUM OF SCOTTISH LIGHTHOUSES ABER/GRAMP

Kinnaird Head, Stevenson Road, Fraserburgh 01346 511 022
www.lighthousemuseum.org.uk
This is a real 'hands-on' museum of quality exhibits that is in no way dull. Lots of buttons and flashing lights for the kids, the story of the lighthouse Stevensons for dad, and remember to help granny climb the stairs of the adjacent lighthouse to see the impressive revolving light and the view of the town.

9 BROUGHTON HOUSE AND GARDEN SOUTH SCOT High Street,

Kirkcudbright 0844 493 2246
www.nts.org.uk/Property/14
The former home of artist E.A. Hornel, this is a delight. As well as viewing paintings, you feel a real insight into his life and times. At the rear there is a Japanese garden that would be worth a visit on its own merits. Now in the ownership of the National Trust for Scotland.

10 DENNY TANK GLAS/CLYDE

Castle Street, Dumbarton
01389 763 444
www.scottishmaritimemuseum.org
Built in 1882, this was used to test models of new ship designs. Despite the demise of Clyde shipbuilding, this facility is still working today. It is as long as a football pitch and you can see models, a design office and other artefacts of shipbuilding as well as eat in the delightful café.

109 DOG-FRIENDLY HOTELS

1 ARDANAISEIG HOTEL WHLLS&T

Kilchrenan, Argyll 01866 833 333
www.ardanaiseig.com
Baronial mansion near the shores of Loch Awe in a remote and dramatic location. Explore the rivers, lochs, craggy peaks and isolated beaches. The Lost Garden that surrounds the house also offers plenty of scope for exploration and quiet contemplation. Dogs are allowed to sleep in the rooms with their owners, although they are not permitted in the public rooms, and there is a dog-sitting service.

2 GREYWALLS HOUSE HOTEL

EDIN/LOTH Gullane, East Lothian
01620 842 144 *www.greywalls.co.uk*
One of Britain's oldest country house hotels in the heart of East Lothian's many great golf courses and bounded by beautiful beaches. Greywalls will happily negotiate accommodation for four-legged friends.

3 CASTLETON HOUSE HOTEL PAD&F

by Glamis, Angus 01307 840 340
www.castleton.co.uk
Four-star country house hotel with a reputation as one of the best places in Scotland for food, ambience and service. Castleton is also near Dundee and Perth, so is ideal as a touring base or as a relaxing holiday location. The expansive grounds are excellent for a morning and evening stroll with the pooch.

4 ST ANDREWS GOLF HOTEL PAD&F

40 The Scores, St Andrews
01334 472 611
www.standrews-golf.co.uk

Combines the feel of a traditional Victorian town house with the luxury and comfort of sumptuous furnishings and fittings. Overlooks the West Sands and historic Old Course and is an ideal base, not only for golf, but from which to explore the many attractions on offer in St Andrews.

5 ROXBURGHE HOTEL AND GOLF COURSE SOUTH SCOT Heiton, by Kelso 01573 450 331 *www.roxburghe.net*
In a prime location for escapism, indulgence and embracing the great outdoors. A number of the hotel's bedrooms have recently been refurbished. Dogs are allowed to stay in the courtyard rooms with their owners, or can take advantage of the hotel's two kennels if required.

110 PLACES TO FLY KITES

1 ISLE OF TIREE WHLLS&T
It's the cream of the kiting world. If Carlsberg made kiting places, they would be very similar to the stunning flat beaches on the island. It is the flatness of Tiree that makes it easy to send kites soaring. There are plenty of on-shore winds and the off-shore winds haven't been tampered with by buildings, which means that there is always a beach with the right directional gust. You can follow on-shore winds right around the island by beach-hopping. Balevullin Bay with its grass half pipe and grass ramps is adventure-tastic and Gott Bay with its clean, clear waters is safe for kite-surfing.

2 NORTH END, WEST SANDS PAD&F
St Andrews
Scotland's premier mainland kiting

location has its very own designated 'kite zone' area which is marked out by council kite flags. The large sandy beach and spacious grassy area are best suited to land board activities. Unfortunately, St Andrews does lack on-shore winds, the smoother kiting winds that come straight off the sea.

3 STEVENSON SOUTH SCOT
Ayrshire
Like St Andrews, the local council in Stevenson are pro-kiting and the area is best for land boarding and buggying. The Scottish Power Kite Association (SPKA) uses Stevenson for racing and freestyle competitions. At Stevenson, the beach is quite narrow, so wind direction has to be suitable even when the tide is out. There is a large park area with hills and paths for exhilarating buggying.

4 BUGHT PARK HIGHLANDS
Inverness
If you are particularly skilful with gusty winds, this inland location is great for kiting from Monday to Saturday, but not on Sundays when the park is full of footballers and their fans. Ideal conditions for kiting in Bught Park are with decent winds from the south-west.

5 LUNAN BAY PAD&F
Angus
A broad east-facing beach of reddish sand backed by dunes and framed by low cliffs. From its northern end near Boddin Point, about three miles south of Montrose, it stretches for over two miles south to Ethie Haven. There's a fair bit of sand here without the traffic or flags. In the middle there is a river, but this can be jumped or passed with a spot of speed.

111 SHOPS TO BUY CHRISTMAS DECORATIONS

1 BONKERS PAD&F
**80 Market Street, St Andrews
01334 473 919**
www.bonkers-standrews.co.uk
Great if you are a student for its wacky gift ideas and cutesy cards, but your mother will like it too as a place to buy classy Christmas decorations. The pieces aren't cheap, but they will still be hanging on the tree years later – and still look wonderful.

2 GERMAN MARKET EDIN/LOTH
The Mound, Edinburgh
For something more unusual to hang on the tree with your tinsel, put down the glühwein for a moment and check out the wares of the little huts. Being hand-made, each piece is unique, and they add a little continental touch to any festive tree. The glassware stall in particular offers lovely choices for those who have smaller trees.

3 JOHN LEWIS
**Edinburgh, Glasgow and Aberdeen
08456 049 049** *www.johnlewis.com*
It's not flash, but John Lewis can be relied on to provide for pretty much any occasion and any budget, an attribute to be treasured at an increasingly crazy time of year. Whether you need boxfuls of basic baubles or a plush penguin that plays a tune, you'll find pretty much everything here – and all without swooning over the price tags.

4 THE PIER
Edinburgh, Glasgow and Aberdeen
0845 609 1234 *www.pier.co.uk*
For something more exotic (the Chinese lantern string of lights catches the eye), or more modern, the Pier is always a good first stop. You can order online until 16 December – great for those who save their tree-trimming until Christmas Eve. It's also the place to check out for candles, whether you want tealights or church candles a foot high.

5 YE OLDE CHRISTMAS SHOPPE
EDIN/LOTH **145 Canongate, Edinburgh
0131 557 9220**
www.scottishchristmas.com
Yes, there's a hint of twee and tartanalia when you step through the door, but then it is the time of year to embrace such things (in fact, you can embrace them any day you care to choose, as this festive emporium is open all year round). The Christmas trees of expats across the globe are surely not complete without a plush Saltire or Scottie dog in a tartan coat dangling from their branches.

112 COUNTRY PARKS

1 VOGRIE COUNTRY PARK
EDIN/LOTH **Pathhead, Midlothian
01875 821 990** *www.midlothian.gov.uk*
A hidden gem, only 12 miles outside Edinburgh city centre, Vogrie has something for everyone. There's a golf course, an epic children's play area, a café inside Vogrie House and a model railway in the summer. But the highlight has to be the range of walks, which take you through woodland and along the side of the River Tyne.

2 MONIKIE COUNTRY PARK PAD&F
Monikie, Angus 01382 370 202
www.angus.gov.uk
Sailing, windsurfing, kayaking and the ropes course are just some of the adventure sports on offer at Monikie Country Park, to the north-east of Dundee. As well as an exciting spot to keep the kids entertained – with instructors on hand to keep everything safe – the park also has a café and large open areas for a kickabout or a picnic. If you need a break from all the excitement, there are a number of quieter walks around Monikie's other reservoirs.

3 LOCHORE MEADOWS COUNTRY PARK PAD&F Lochgelly, Fife
01592 414 300
www.lochore-meadows.co.uk
A great example of how the countryside can be reclaimed from an old industrial landscape, Lochore Meadows was once a colliery.
Fife Council runs an outdoor education centre from the park and the site also includes a trout fishery and a golf course. But it's the walks around the 1,200-acre park that are best – there's also a bird hide at the west end of the loch, inside a nature reserve.

4 CHATELHERAULT COUNTRY PARK
GLAS/CLYDE **Hamilton, South Lanarkshire**
www.southlanarkshire.gov.uk
You could spend a whole day at Chatelherault and still not see everything – the Duke of Hamilton's hunting lodge, designed by William Adam, is excellent, as are the beautiful gorge walks along Avon Water – plus there are rare white cattle to watch roaming the park.

5 ALMONDELL AND CALDERWOOD COUNTRY PARK EDIN/LOTH
Mid Calder, West Lothian
www.westlothian.gov.uk
The walks along the banks of the River Almond are one of the highlights of a visit to Almondell and Calderwood Country Park. The visitor centre has information about the two former estates and the area's geology. Always popular at weekends but quieter during the week.

113 EDIN-BURGERS

1 WANNABURGER EDIN/LOTH
217 High St 0131 225 8770 *and*
7/8 Queensferry St, Edinburgh
0131 220 0036 *www.wannaburger.com*
Claiming to be Edinburgh's best burger restaurant company, it is difficult to disagree for two reasons. One is The Aussie – truly a king among burgers. Created with your choice of chicken fillet, beef or veggie pattie, layered with mature cheddar, a slice of fresh pineapple, beetroot, salad and crowned with a fried egg. You will find no other burger like it. Two, the Peanut Butter and Banana smoothie. Put these two together and you have a meal that will satisfy you for the rest of the day.

2 ALL BAR ONE EDIN/LOTH
50 Lothian Road, Edinburgh
0131 221 7951
Yes, it's a chain, and as such tends to come in for a bit of stick – but their homemade beefburger is tremendous. Thick and chunky, stuffed with fresh herbs and chopped onion, it comes as a juicy taste explosion with a choice of toppings and a massive plate of thin chips.

3 THE CAMBRIDGE BAR EDIN/LOTH
20 Young Street, Edinburgh
0131 226 2120
www.thecambridgebar.co.uk
Whether it's the blue cheese burger, a dish in which large hunks of stilton melt down onto a 100 per cent Scottish beefburger, or the more girly option of chargrilled chicken with salad and mayo, The Cambridge Bar is heaven. Enjoyed by city suits during the week, it's much more laid back at the weekends when you can stumble in with hangovers and discuss last night's antics over a bowl of chunky chips.

4 HECTORS EDIN/LOTH
47–49 Deanhaugh Street, Stockbridge, Edinburgh
An outstanding thick (and really home-made) burger, halved and served on a more unusual long breadbun, and best of all served ungarnished so you can make those important decisions yourself.

5 BLUE MOON CAFÉ EDIN/LOTH
36 Broughton Street, Edinburgh
Again, a truly home-made monster hamburger. Heavy on the garlic and onion spices, and served with a very non-modest portion of chips. Very busy most of the time.

114 COASTAL PAINTERS

1 WILLIAM McTAGGART
McTaggart painted the sea like no-one else. He regularly visited the Kintyre harbours and shores of Campbeltown, Machrihanish and Carradale. Storms, herring boats, fisher children abound in his art; sometimes just a big sea,

calm or pulsing with the vibrant energy of nature. His 1890 masterpiece, *The Storm*, was painted in the garden of his Carradale house overlooking the bay. Look long enough at these great impressionistic seascapes and you'll smell the salt air and watch the waves roll.

2 JOHN BELLANY
Bellany was born and brought up in Port Seton in the 1940s. The small East Lothian harbour is still active and its fishing boats and local people appear in these paintings produced throughout his (still-prolific) career. There are strange fish, grotesque crustaceans and ravening birds but more sunshiny-yellow optimism in his latter years.

3 LS LOWRY
Berwick is, of course, an honorary Scottish town. Lowry is more often associated with matchstick men (and cats and dogs) against a background of smoking Lancashire mills. But he often spent holidays in Berwick, painting and drawing the town and coast.

4 JOAN EARDLEY
Eardley lived in Catterline, a small former fishing village near Stonehaven from 1956 until her death in 1963. She produced many paintings of the area, the thickly-layered paint creating richly textured surfaces and often capturing violent weather effects on sea and land. What a contrast with her depictions of Glasgow street children.

5 THE REV JOHN THOMSON
Fast Castle is a dramatic ruin on a sheer cliff above the North Sea near St Abb's Head, Berwickshire. Thomson (who, in the little time he could spare from

painting, ministered to his Duddingston parishioners) is best remembered for his numerous early 19th century canvases of this site. Forget about surface cracks and dodgy technique – just delight in the sun glinting and shimmering through louring storm-clouds onto the tempest-tossed sea and spotlighting the disintegrating fastness atop its eyrie crag.

115 CHEAP GOLF HOTELS

1 THE UDNY ARMS ABER/GRAMP
Newburgh, Aberdeenshire
01358 789 444 *www.udny.co.uk*
Despite now being a chain-owned hotel, the Udny Arms still maintains the family-run feeling. It is handily placed for Cruden Bay, Newmachar, Murcar and many other wonderful golf courses. Whether eating in the restaurant or the bar, cuisine is superb and cask-ale drinkers will never be disappointed here.

2 SOUTH BEACH HOTEL SOUTH SCOT
Troon, Ayrshire 01292 312 033
www.southbeach.co.uk
The South Beach is the ideal base for anyone golfing in Ayrshire: Troon, Prestwick, Irvine – and Turnberry if you want to pay the prices – are all within easy reach. Accommodation is very comfortable and the restaurant offers a good range of locally sourced produce.

3 THE PORTCULLIS WHLLS&T
Castle Wynd, Stirling 01786 472 290
www.theportcullishotel.com
Situated beside Stirling Castle, this might seem a strange choice of 'golf hotel' but, with the proximity of the motorways, most of Scotland's top

courses are within an hour's drive. Add the benefits of staying in the city of Stirling itself and you have found an ideal holiday or short-break venue. One word of caution though: the standard of cuisine is superb, but the piled platefuls could seriously damage your waistline!

4 THE SCORES HOTEL PAD&F
76 The Scores, St Andrews, Fife 01334 472 451 *www.scoreshotel.co.uk*
If location, location, location is your thing, then this cannot be beaten. Literally a long putt or a thinned chip from the hallowed 18th green on the Old Course, the Scores offers comfortable accommodation and good food at prices that, if not the cheapest, are more affordable than the likes of the Old Course Hotel.

5 NEW HALL PAD&F
North Haugh, St Andrews University, St Andrews, Fife 01334 462 000
www.escapetotranquillity.com
If St Andrews is the Mecca of golf, maybe a choice of accommodation is appropriate. Outwith term-time, the university makes its student accommodation available to Joe Public. The rooms in New Hall are well-appointed and well-maintained: some students these days enjoy facilities that are hugely superior to those experienced by previous generations.

116 PLACES FOR STEAM ENTHUSIASTS

1 STRATHSPEY STEAM RAILWAY
HIGHLANDS **Aviemore to Broomhill via Boat of Garten 01479 810 725**
www.strathspeysteamrailway.co.uk

If the sun comes out and the rain stops then there's no place to rival the Spey Valley. Gazing up at the majestic Cairngorms is a real treat when your journey is accompanied by the whistle of the steam engine and the clouds of smoke fanning out above the train. While you wait for the engine to turn round at Broomhill, take a walk along the platform and have your photo taken beside the sign for Glenbogle Station, Broomhill's *Monarch Of The Glen* alter-ego. One day, the line may take in a fourth station and run up to Grantown-on-Spey.

2 BO'NESS AND KINNEIL RAILWAY

EDIN/LOTH Bo'ness Station, Union Street, Bo'ness 01506 822 298
www.srps.org.uk/railway
The Scottish Railway Preservation Society operates the Bo'ness and Kinneil Railway by the south shore of the Firth of Forth. Several historic buildings have been obtained and re-erected to provide a traditional railway setting. Bo'ness station opened in 1981, and a passenger service now operates to Birkhill, where the fireclay mine is now open to the public. The SRPS operates trains pulled by both steam and diesel locomotives and there are regular events aimed at children, such as Easter specials and Thomas the Tank Engine weekends.

3 MODEL RAIL SCOTLAND EXHIBITION GLAS/CLYDE

Scottish Exhibition and Conference Centre, Glasgow *(every February)*
www.modelrail-scotland.co.uk
Scotland's model railway clubs come together for their annual jamboree, which is a must for rail enthusiasts, and a hit with children.

4 JACOBITE STEAM TRAIN

HIGHLANDS Fort William to Mallaig 01524 737 751 *www.steamtrain.info*
Needs little introduction, given its association with Harry Potter films. It is one of the greatest railway journeys in the world.

5 NATIONAL RAILWAY MUSEUM,

Leeman Road, York 08704 214 001
www.nrm.org.uk
OK, so it's not in Scotland, but it's still the mecca for rail enthusiasts. It's the world's largest railway museum and includes a replica of Stephenson's 1829 Rocket and a Flying Scotsman exhibition.

117 CAFÉS

1 THE HUB AT GLENTRESS SOUTH

SCOT Glentress Forest, near Peebles, Scottish Borders
www.thehubintheforest.co.uk
The Hub Café is just that: a vibrant hub to relax in with a plate of good food after a long day in the hills taking on the many different mountain bike and walking trails that run for miles around. They focus their efforts on home-cooked food and a welcoming environment guaranteeing a great atmosphere with a great mix of people from all ages.

2 REAL FOOD CAFÉ WHLLS&T

Main Street, Tyndrum, Argyll
www.therealfoodcafe.com
At the halfway point of the West Highland Way, this is a haven for many walkers exploring the spectacular and remote environment. Supplied by local produce and renowned for amazing fish and chips and well as home-made muesli and burgers made from locally-reared cattle.

3 THE WATERMILL AT ABERFELDY

PAD&F **Mill Street, Aberfeldy**
www.aberfeldywatermill.com
The largest bookshop in the rural
Highlands, stocking over 5,000 titles,
the old watermill has been restored
into a great space for settling down
into a comfy sofa, taking advantage of
the relaxed environment. Another
option would be to browse through the
books and gallery until your heart is
content or your stomach is empty, then
head to the coffee shop to have a well
earned cup of tea/smoothie and snack.

4 SKOON ART CAFÉ OUT. ISLES

4 Geocrab, Isle of Harris
www.skoon.com
Gorgeous food, beautiful interior, great
local art for sale, books to read while
eating and all the food is organic.
A traditional croft renovated into a
modern café/gallery with a changing
menu which makes the most of local
produce.

5 MOUNTAIN CAFÉ HIGHLANDS

111 Grampian Road, Aviemore
www.mountaincafe-aviemore.co.uk
A favourite with the adventurers,
situated above the adventure clothing
shop the café is a great place to relax
amongst the buzz of activity, and with
excellent servings of home baking you
can start the exercise plan after a
mound of chocolate cake.

118 COASTAL WALKS

1 THE FIFE COASTAL PATH PAD&F

www.fifecoastalpath.co.uk
What a beautiful start in North
Queensferry, with the awe-inspiring
architecture of the Forth Bridge
looming overhead and the views of
Arthur's Seat and Edinburgh beyond.
A great way to find out more of
Scotland's history, from the ancient and
mysterious prehistoric art of Wemyss
Caves through to the Kirkcaldy
promenade, which was built as an
employment project during a period of
depression. All the while the beauty of
the cliffs and the sea dominate this
long-distance path.

2 STONEHAVEN PROMENADE AND CLIFF WALK ABER/GRAMP

www.stonehavenguide.net
The beautiful views across the harbour
bring people to this town from across
Europe and further afield. Of particular
interest is the site of the oldest animal
fossil find in Britain, and the Highland
fault. Further along the coast,
Dunnottar Castle dominates the skyline.

3 CULLEN TO SPEY BAY

ABER/GRAMP
www.speysideway.org
www.moray.gov.uk and
www.wdcs.org/wildlifecentre
Incorporates the Moray Coastal Path
and the start of the Speyside Way.
This day's walking starts with dramatic
cliff scenery, goes through historic
fishing villages and ends at the estuary
of the River Spey. The Tugnet Ice House
and associated natural history
interpretive centre at the end of this
walk are well worth visiting. On a good
day, dolphins can be seen swimming in
the Moray Firth.

4 ARBROATH TO SEATON CLIFFS

PAD&F *www.swt.org.uk*
The main path, maintained and owned
by the Scottish Wildlife Trust, provides

an excellent viewing point for the majestic old red sandstone cliffs of this area. There are great views across to St Andrews and watch out for a display by local porpoises. Combine this with a visit to Arbroath Abbey and its excellent visitor centre. Make sure you try a delicious Arbroath smokie before you finish your day.

5 OBAN PROMENADE AND BAY
WHLLS&T *www.oban.org.uk*
Excellent views across towards Mull. The grace of the Calmac ferry moving across the bay – urging all to visit the Isle of Mull and go on to the spiritual haven of Iona – adds to the sense of peace in this busy and popular seaside town. This is an excellent start or finish to a day at this west coast resort.

119 INTRIGUING PLACE NAMES

1 JEMIMAVILLE HIGHLANDS
Several places are named after their creator's wife. None, surely, as delightfully as this Black Isle village on the B9163 near Cromarty.

2 AUCHTERMUCHTY PAD&F
I used to think it was a couthie version of the exotic Timbuktu, both mythical places. Now I know one is in Mali and the other in Fife (on the A91 to/from Cupar) and was the location for the 1990s *Dr Finlay's Casebook* (not the original series, which was set in Callander).

3 MAGGIEKNOCKATER ABER/GRAMP
The Road to Maggieknockater (which is probably the A95 unless you live very locally) is a book on North East place

names by Robert Smith, prolific chronicler of the area's curiosities. There was no Maggie Knockater.

4 KITTYBREWSTER ABER/GRAMP
This area of Aberdeen used to be covered with railway stations, marshalling yards and a cattle market. Now there are retail parks. There was no Kitty Brewster.

5 DRUMNADROCHIT HIGHLANDS
On Loch Ness (on the A82 near Urquhart Castle), this is the site of Wild Goose... sorry, Loch Ness Monster... Exhibitions. One's the Original, and the other the Official, Monster Exhibition. There is no Loch Ness Monster (allegedly).

6 PORTKNOCKIE ABER/GRAMP
Former Moray fishing village, site of the Bow Fiddle Rock, a large sea arch resembling – yes, that's right – the bow of a fiddle. On the A942 to the north-east of Buckie.

7 PORTMAHOMACK HIGHLANDS
This Sutherland fishing village (at the end of the B9165 looking over the Dornoch Firth) has been home since 1989 to the highly productive writer of Victorian mysteries Anne Perry and a wonderful Pictish museum.

8 ARDNAMURCHAN HIGHLANDS
Suitably harsh-sounding name for the remote peninsula whose point is the westernmost on the British mainland (except for the finicky whose preference is for Corrachadh Mor, a km south and a gnat's leap further west). Long, winding drive along the B8007, then onto a road even more minor than that.

9 ACHILTIBUIE HIGHLANDS
North of Ullapool (west off the A835 at
Drumrunie and follow a minor road
round past Loch Osgaig), this village of
white-washed cottages is best known
for the Hydroponicum, where plants are
grown without soil.

10 ROSEHEARTY ABER/GRAMP
An optimistic name for a pleasant
village along the B9031 coast road
going west from Fraserburgh. Much
better than 'the wood of Abterach',
the literal translation of the original
Gaelic name.

120 PLACES TO BUY CHRISTMAS CARDS

1 PAPER TIGER EDIN/LOTH
53 Lothian Road and **6 Stafford Street,
Edinburgh, 0131 228 2790/226 2390**
www.papertiger.ltd.uk
A great source of unusual cards all year
round, Paper Tiger comes into its own
for the festive season. Whether you
want a stack of boxes or just the one
for that special someone, you'll find just
the right card in here. Perfect for
anyone who likes their humour more
cerebral than lavatorial.

2 PAPYRUS GLAS/CLYDE
374 Byres Road and **Buchanan Galleries,
Glasgow 0141 334 6514/332 6788**
www.papyrusgifts.co.uk
A treasure trove of quirkiness, stylish
and offbeat envelope-fillers. The city-
centre branch is handier, but the West
End original is fractionally quieter and
more conducive to browsing. Perfect for
hip friends and funky younger relatives.

3 ROYAL MUSEUM EDIN/LOTH
Chambers Street, Edinburgh
0131 225 7534 *www.nms.ac.uk*
The shop has been exiled to the main
hall during renovations, but still has all
its usual goodies. It has a wide range of
cards, with a good selection of more
thoughtful designs and some religious
imagery. Perfect for the older
generation or those who lament the
commercialisation of Christmas.

4 DOBBIES EDIN/LOTH
Melville Nursery Lasswade, Midlothian
0131 663 1941 *www.dobbies.com*
I can happily spend a couple of hours in
Dobbies, and one of the reasons is their
range of Christmas cards.
Unsurprisingly, there are lots of wildlife
and nature images, but what's not to
like about a robin perched on a snow-
dusted garden spade? Perfect for the
gardener and birdwatcher in your life.
See website for locations of other
Dobbies at Ayr, Cumbernauld, Dalgety
Bay, Dunfermline, Dundee, Kinross,
Milngavie, Paisley, Perth and Stirling.

5 ST JOHN'S CHURCH, EDIN/LOTH
Edinburgh and charity shops
everywhere *www.cardsforcharity.co.uk*
Obvious, but true: charities get a better
cut of the money from your Christmas
card purchase if you buy them as
directly as possible. Browse at the shop
of your choice, or visit St John's Church
on Princes Street, which hosts 'Cards for
Good Causes', run by volunteers. Cards
from around two dozen charities are
available to buy, with at least 80p of
every £1 going to the charity.

121 WATERFALLS

1 EAS A' CHUAL ALUINN HIGHLANDS

Reached via boat from Kylesku or on foot along the shore of Loch Glencoul or via the appropriately named Bealach a' Bhuirich (the roaring pass), this is the UK's highest waterfall, dropping more than 200 m down the rocky precipice of Leitir Dhubh. The falls are sometimes known by the folk name of the Maiden's Tresses in memory of an apocryphal maiden who threw herself off the cliff rather than be with a man she did not love, her trailing tresses forming the falls.

2 THE FALLS OF MEASACH

HIGHLANDS

Some 12 miles south of Ullapool and in the care of the National Trust for Scotland since 1945, this is one of Scotland's best-known and renowned falls due in no small measure to their ease of access. They fall into the spectacular wooded gorge of Corrieshalloch, 'the filthy hollow', and can be reached by means of only a short walk from either of two main roads. Yet even in season, it is possible to have them all to yourself.

3 FALLS OF GLOMACH HIGHLANDS

These are located in the oft neglected back yard of the magnificent Five Sister mountains of Kintail, about 18 miles east of Kyle of Lochalsh. Access to the falls is difficult and potentially dangerous and it involves an arduous tramp over rough and remote countryside. But perseverance is well-rewarded.

4 AN STEALL BAN HIGHLANDS

Located in Upper Glen Nevis above the dramatic Nevis Gorge, sometimes referred to as 'Himalayan' and to many, the most outstanding gorge in Scotland. Not to be outdone, An Steall Ban, the white spout, is itself regarded by many as the finest waterfall in Scotland.

5 LEALT FALLS HIGHLANDS

Situated in north-east Skye, on the road from Portree to Staffin. Easily accessible from the roadside car park down a steep and often treacherous path. However, the best view is reserved for those who approach from the sea when the spectacular falls are seen in all their glory, backed by the weird and stunning rock formations of the Trotternish Ridge.

122 PLACES TO FEED DUCKS

1 BRODIE CASTLE ABER/GRAMP

near Forres, Moray 0844 493 2156
www.nts.org.uk
Come rain or shine, the swans, mallards and tufted ducks on the pond at Brodie Castle are always happy to relieve you of any stale bread. You don't even have to pay the entrance fee for the Moray castle as the pond has its own tiny car park. If it's wet and you want to sit and watch the birds, then visit one of the hides.

2 BROUGHTY FERRY PAD&F

Dundee *www.cometobroughty.co.uk*
With more swans than you can shake a crust at – plus gulls and mallards – Broughty Ferry is top of the seaside duck-feeding list. The best spot is on Beach Crescent, where the swans usually gather on the small strip of shoreline between the jetty and

harbour wall. The nearby chip shop and ice-cream parlour add to the magic.

3 MUSSELBURGH EDIN/LOTH
East Lothian
The River Esk, which runs through Musselburgh, is teeming with bird life. For superior duck-feeding, shy away from the car park at Eskside East – instead, opt for a vantage point on the footbridge further downstream, where you can at least try to avoid some of the seagulls, and feed the local mallards, swans, Canada geese and greylag geese.

4 ST ANDREWS PAD&F
Fife *www.visit-standrews.co.uk*
A quiet refuge for many students down the years, the Kinnesburn, which flows through St Andrews, offers a chance for some contemplative duck-feeding. When you reach the foot of Queen's Gardens, cross Queen's Terrace and head down the travellator steps towards Kinnesburn Road. Mallards gather around the footbridge, ever hopeful of a spare slice.

5 FORRES ABER/GRAMP
Moray *www.forresweb.net*
The Duck Pond in Forres has been a favourite with generations of local children. The town has enjoyed success in both the Scotland in Bloom and Britain in Bloom competition since the 1970s. It is well worth having a wander around Grant Park, complete with its Sunken Garden and Rose Garden.

123 DOG WALKING

1 HERMITAGE OF BRAID EDIN/LOTH
Edinburgh
According to at least one greyhound,

the best-ever dog-walking venue is the Hermitage of Braid and Blackford Hill. This beautiful nature reserve has it all: rolling hills where rabbits lurk under gorse bushes, open fields, shady woods and a stream. Best of all, though, is the number of friendly, well-socialised pooches – plenty of opportunities for bottom-sniffing, competitive peeing and playing chase (and the dogs have fun too).

2 TENTSMUIR PAD&F
Near Leuchars
A few miles down a single-track road from Leuchars is this wonderful beach, bounded by forest. It lies on a spit, at the point of which is a fenced-off nature reserve where dogs must be kept on the lead. The rest is unrestricted though – the beach is especially good for high-energy hounds who will enjoy a good run along the sands. The forest has long, shady pathways and freshwater ditches for the dog if you have forgotten to bring a drink. The car park, which costs £1, has a picnic and barbecue area but no litter bins – you must pack your rubbish and dispose of it at home.

3 LONGNIDDRY BENTS EDIN/LOTH
East Lothian
Excellent spot to take the kids and the dog. A lovely big curving beach with rocks and rockpools, rivulets, dunes and woodland on the edge for exploring.

4 STIRLING GOLF COURSE WHLLS&T
A perfect hour's walk around the outside of the course. The dog gets to bother rabbits who wait tantalisingly until they are almost caught before popping down their burrows and the owner gets fabulous views of the castle

and the Stirling skyline – and the opportunity to laugh at the bad golfers.

5 BROUGHTY FERRY PAD&F

The beach at Broughty Ferry is a beautiful spot and quiet, particularly in winter, with great views of the Tay firth and lovely seaweedy smells for Rover.

6 MUGDOCK COUNTRY PARK

GLAS/CLYDE near Milngavie, East Dunbartonshire

Great for dogs who love to run through muddy puddles and sniff trees.

7 BALLOCH COUNTRY PARK

WHLLS&T Balloch

Excellent if your dog likes a swim as the water is very clean and there's lots of open grass for a good game of chase the stick.

124 À LA CARTE EATING

1 THE VILLAGE INN WHLLS&T

Long Loch, Arrochar, Argyll
01301 702 458 *www.maclay.com*
One of the most beautiful settings for outdoor dining in Scotland. At the heart of the Loch Lomond and Trossachs National Park, the grounds enjoy stunning views of the 'Arrochar Alps' and Loch Long. The menu is simple, home-cooked pub food, which is hearty, tasty and enhanced by the scenery.

2 HILTON DUNKELD HOUSE PAD&F

Dunkeld 01350 727 771
www.hilton.co.uk/dunkeld
A haven in rural Perthshire with personality and character. It has an idyllic location on the banks of the River Tay and acres of grounds to wander through. Its à la carte dining

menu doesn't disappoint and includes char-grilled sirloin steak for the hungry and a selection of seasonal salads and sandwiches for the peckish.

3 HOUSE FOR AN ART LOVER

GLAS/CLYDE Bellahouston Park, Glasgow 0141 353 4770
www.houseforanartlover.co.uk
Not only one of Glasgow's top tourist and cultural attractions; it also has one of the finest restaurants in the city with beautiful views over Bellahouston Park. It has an extensive and well-thought-out à la carte menu including some impressive seafood options, such as Dublin Bay prawns, fillet of red mullet and seared scallops.

4 THE KILTED SKIRLIE WHLLS&T

Loch Lomond Shores, Balloch
01389 754 759 *www.kiltedskirlie.co.uk*
Loch Lomond stretched out beneath the terrace provides a picture postcard of a view and, if that's not enough to hold your attention, then the promenade is a hub of activity, boasting farmers' markets and live music. This is, without doubt, one to treat your out-of-town relatives to and, with plenty of child friendly activity on the shores, ideal for all the family.

5 THE FORTH FLOOR RESTAURANT

EDIN/LOTH Harvey Nichols, St Andrews Square, Edinburgh 0131 524 8350
www.harveynichols.com
Affords spectacular views across the city and is a real slice of cosmopolitan life. Tablecloths and suited waiters give a sophisticated air to outdoor dining but, surprisingly, the prices don't break the bank. It's an ideal respite from shopping.

125 LAND-BASED DOLPHIN WATCHING

There are five species of dolphin regularly found in Scottish waters: the short-beaked common, white-beaked, Atlantic white-sided, Risso's and bottlenose. While watching dolphins is often about 'right time, right place', Scotland boasts some excellent land-based vantage points. August is the ideal month to search from the shore, as the sea is flat and visibility good.

1 ABERDEEN HARBOUR
ABER/GRAMP *Grid Ref NJ 952050*
www.aberdeen-harbour.co.uk
The calm waters of the harbour may not seem to be the most promising of locations, but schools of dolphins are reported regularly around the entrance. Habituated to boat traffic, dolphins are frequently seen bow-riding and breaching. Alongside bottlenose, the more pelagic white-beaked is a visitor in the summer.

2 ARDNAMURCHAN POINT
HIGHLANDS *Grid Ref NM 416674*
www.ardnamurchan.u-net.com
While it takes considerable effort (about 30 miles of single-track road) to reach mainland Britain's (arguably) most westerly point, the Ardnamurchan Peninsula, the effort is well worth it. This is a wild, desolate, dramatic and beautiful place. The 36 m lighthouse has been converted into a visitor centre, open April until September.

3 CHANONRY POINT HIGHLANDS
Black Isle *Grid Ref NH 749557*
In truth, there are several locations on the Black Isle easy to recommend, but Chanonry Point at the end of a long

spit of land between Fortrose and Rosemarkie, is legendary among dolphin-watchers. The majority of dolphins encountered belong to the most northerly resident population of bottlenose dolphins on the planet.

4 MULL OF OA WHLLS&T
Islay *Grid Ref NR 282423*
www.rspb.org.uk
The sheer cliffs of the southern headland of Islay, the Mull of Oa, are an excellent vantage point for dolphin-watching. On a clear day, the Mull of Oa provides great views of the Antrim coast and out into the Atlantic Ocean.

5 SPEY BAY ABER/GRAMP
Moray *Grid Ref NJ 325657*
www.swt.org.uk
Spey Bay Wildlife Reserve is one of the largest vegetated areas of shingle beach in Scotland. The main attraction is bottlenose dolphins leaping often only metres from the shore. Although the wildlife reserve is managed by the Scottish Wildlife Trust, the Whale and Dolphin Conservation Society has a visitor centre adjacent to the reserve.

126 GARDEN CENTRES

1 SMEATON NURSERY & GARDENS
EDIN/LOTH **Smeaton, East Linton**
01620 860 501
At the end of a long, tree-lined driveway, a door in a wall opens, secret-garden-like. Behind it is the entrance to a walled garden beautifully clad with fruit trees and filled with avenues of plants. It has an atmosphere from another era: you half expect to bump into Lady Chatterley's Mellors pushing a

barrow. Knowledgeable staff are on hand to talk plants.

2 MERRYHATTON GARDEN CENTRE
EDIN/LOTH **East Fortune, North Berwick, East Lothian 01620 880 278**
www.merryhatton.co.uk
Another hidden gem off the beaten track, in this case, the B1377. Merryhatton, a working nursery, holds an excellent stock, particularly for alpines, and a seasonal herb range with over 200 varieties. It is also great for picking up something different in garden hardware and ornaments.

3 PENTLAND PLANTS EDIN/LOTH
Loanhead, Midlothian *(on the A701, 400 yards past Ikea)* **0131 440 0895**
www.pentlandplants.co.uk
Family-run business with a large stock including the season's must-haves for the garden. If you're after a chocolate cosmos, this is the place to head for. You'll find plenty of ideas and advice on how to make your garden sing. One of the family is Carolyn Spray, of the BBC's *Beechgrove Garden*.

4 JACK DRAKE'S INSHRIACH NURSERY HIGHLANDS **near Aviemore 01540 651287** *www.drakesalpines.com*
Four recommendations for one venue. It's a rock and alpine garden, a nursery with an amazing range of rare plants, a tearoom – and it has a viewing gallery to watch red squirrels. It is situated between Loch Insh Watersports and Coylumbridge on the B970.

5 NEW HOPETOUN GARDENS
EDIN/LOTH **Newton, West Lothian 01506 834 433**
www.newhopetoungardens.co.uk
Keep a firm grip on your wallet in this wonderful garden centre, or you could find yourself dazedly queuing with a trolley-load. There are separate sections for roses, bedding plants, alpines, vegetables, fruit trees and herbs, while shrubs and perennials are arranged alphabetically. More expensive than most but definitely worth it.

127 LOCHS

1 LOCH ETCHACHAN HIGHLANDS
Cairngorms
Nestling beneath the summit of Ben MacDui, Britain's second highest mountain, Loch Etchachan is the highest in the UK at over 3,000 ft above sea level. Perhaps the best way to come upon the loch is to approach Ben MacDui from Glen Derry on a louring winter day. The icy surface has a chilling beauty of another world.

2 LOCH MAREE HIGHLANDS
Assynt
The very name of Loch Maree evokes the breathtaking loveliness of Scotland's west coast sea lochs. Cutting deep into the mountains of the mainland, Loch Maree's beauty is nowhere more evident than from the winding road on its western shore. Wild and lovely Slioch dominates the windswept waters.

3 LOCH SHIEL HIGHLANDS
Lochaber
The Glenfinnan Monument, where Bonnie Prince Charlie raised the Jacobite standard in 1745, marks the head of stunningly attractive Loch Shiel. The loch is perhaps most beautiful on an evening in late summer, when high clouds scud across the sky.

4 LOCH ERICHT HIGHLANDS
Lochaber
The most striking view of lovely Loch Ericht is from the summit of Beinn Bheoil. A long 16-mile walk or cycle from the arterial A9 road, this shapely mountain is best climbed along with neighbouring Ben Alder. As the summit is reached the wild and remote stretch of water that is Loch Ericht springs into view in all its glory.

5 LOCH AVON HIGHLANDS
Cairngorms
The vast Arctic plateau of the Cairngorms has so many wonderful and remote lochs that naming the best one is very difficult, but Loch Avon is surely one of the most beautiful. It fills the tract of land between Cairngorm and Beinn Mheadoin and the walk between the two mountains is undoubtedly one of the best views to be found in mountaineering anywhere in Scotland.

128 SCULPTURES

1 VULCAN EDIN/LOTH
National Gallery of Modern Art, Belford Road, Edinburgh 0131 624 6200
www.nationalgalleries.org
Paolozzi's steel portrayal of the god of fire is stunning, from its shiny toes to the tip of the hammer seven metres above. Its craftsmanship makes it a fitting tribute to a god of blacksmiths and sculptors. Walk around his feet (different sizes, as Vulcan was said to be lame) and then go up to the gallery's first-floor balcony to gaze into his face.

2 GIRAFFES EDIN/LOTH
Omni Centre, Picardy Place, Edinburgh
Their official name is Dreaming Spires, but artist Helen Dennerly christened the giraffe mother and son Martha and Gilbert. Constructed from motorbike and car parts, they could represent concerns about recycling. They bring a touch of African sun to grey Edinburgh.

3 MILLENNIUM CLOCK EDIN/LOTH
Royal Museum, Chambers Street, Edinburgh 0131 247 4422
www.nms.ac.uk
Every time you look at this piece, you will see something different – and that's even when not watching it chime. Whether you take it face value as a kinetic sculpture, or delve into its workings and find the significance of the figures represented on its many levels, this is an astonishing piece.

4 THE HEAVY HORSE GLAS/CLYDE
Glasgow Business Park
www.scottsculptures.co.uk
Unveiled in 1997, this work by Andy Scott has heads turning on the M8. Although it looks like a wire-mesh folly, the four-metre-high sculpture is made of galvanised steel bars, even in its construction pointing out the clash between beauty and strength embodied in the Clydesdale horse, originally bred in Lanarkshire. Its inspiration was apparently Glasgow itself.

5 COMMANDO MONUMENT
HIGHLANDS **Spean Bridge**
Where does sculpture end and monument begin? This is certainly a moving example of the latter, but also a fine example of the former. The three soldiers on their plinth have for 55 years looked out over the hills to Ben Nevis and Aonach Mor, the commandos' training ground after the force's creation in 1940. The detail of their

uniforms is excellent, but look up into their faces and you will see the artist's skill most clearly. They gaze into the distance with a look of both determination and resignation.

129 RUNS

1 BRAIDS AND BLACKFORD HILL
EDIN/LOTH **Edinburgh**
Take the bridle path that winds through the golf course up to the summit of the Braid Hills. Sweeping views over the Forth from the Bridges to Bass Rock and everything in between will take your already ragged breath away. Head to Blackford Hill through the peaceful Hermitage of Braid. Banish wobbly bits by building in some of the steps and steeper inclines around Blackford – especially the killer staircase on the west face.

2 LEWS CASTLE GROUNDS OUT.
ISLES **Stornoway, Isle of Lewis**
Follow the path that winds around the coast – the view stretches across Stornoway to the harbour and the start of the Eye Peninsula. Choose any of a number of shaded woodland paths to take you inland. Climb up to top of Gallows Hill to see the chambered cairn before running back toward the derelict castle and finally back to town.

3 ISLAY WHLLS&T
Almost every one who passes you running on Islay's quiet roads will gee you on with a toot of the horn or a shout of encouragement. Long sandy beaches, like Machir Bay, or those around Loch Gruinart give calf muscles a tough workout. Finish with a cool-down jog through the chilly Atlantic surf. But the best thing about running

on Islay comes later – a couple of tots of single malt.

4 GIGHA WHLLS&T
At just seven miles from north to south, you can run the length of the island in about an hour with a delicious sea breeze to keep you cool. Gentle inclines and nothing too arduous, the sensational views over to the Kintyre peninsula and, on a clear day, across to Northern Ireland as well as the occasional glimpse of a seal will keep you distracted.

5 OCEAN TERMINAL TO CRAMOND LOOP EDIN/LOTH **Edinburgh**
Pace yourself on the flat, fast Forthside half-marathon course. Race around the docks and take in the urban regeneration around Granton and Trinity, through to Silverknowes. Around the halfway mark, there's an exhilarating downhill stretch with a great view over the Forth to Cramond island and Fife. Loop back along the promenade to Leith and don't forgot to clock your time.

130 THAI FOOD

1 THAI CAFÉ OUT. ISLES
27 Church Street, Stornoway, Lewis
01851 701 811
Finding tasty Thai cuisine in the capital of the Hebrides may come as a surprise, but this fusion of East meets Western Isles (garlic meets Gaelic?) uses the finest local produce, especially seafood. Try the pad ped thalay, wonderfully tasty prawns and mussels with red curry paste and peppers. And for those who like it hot, order the Thai Café hot pan – marinated chicken stir-fried with peppers, mushrooms, ginger and lots of

garlic – which comes sizzling to the table. Booking is highly recommended, and take your own wine (there is a corkage charge).

2 DUSIT EDIN/LOTH
49a Thistle Street, Edinburgh
0131 220 6846
A very different Thai experience – strong contemporary feel with imported spices fused with the best fresh Scottish produce. The result is high-quality food with lots of unexpected twists to the traditional Thai menu. Favoured by business types buttering up clients and contacts.

3 LANNA THAI EDIN/LOTH
32 Bridge Street, Musselburgh
0131 653 2788 and **19 Queensgate, Inverness** HIGHLANDS **01463 226 644**
A little gem that not many people outside of Musselburgh seem to know about. It is a small but exquisitely decorated family-run restaurant with über-friendly service and fabulous food. Their Thai wine and beer is not half bad either. Can be hard to get a table at weekends, but the takeaway service is good and you never get a bad meal.

4 SONGKRAN EDIN/LOTH
24a Stafford Street, Edinburgh
0131 225 7889
Tiny wee restaurant hidden away in a basement, which serves consistently high-quality food. It's a great place for a rendezvous. There is a Songkran II not far away at 8 Gloucester Street in the New Town.

5 AYUTTHAYA EDIN/LOTH
148 Nicolson Street, Edinburgh
0131 556 9351
A bit dark and tight for space, but this

adds to the charm of this atmospheric little place near the Festival Theatre, with good service and lovely grub.

131 PLACES TO SEE RARE BUTTERFLIES

1 ALLT MHUIC NATURE RESERVE
HIGHLANDS **Inverness-shire**
Grid Ref NN 121912
www.butterfly-conservation.org
Butterfly Conservation's first nature reserve in Scotland was opened in 2003. Allt Mhuic boasts an immensely enjoyable two-mile circular way-marked trail through woodland, rough grassland and open moorland. It supports substantial populations of three of Scotland's rarer butterflies – chequered skipper, pearl-bordered fritillary and small pearl-bordered fritillary.

2 BEN LAWERS NATIONAL NATURE RESERVE PAD&F **Perthshire** *Grid Ref 608379 www.nnr-scotland.org.uk*
At 1,214 m, Ben Lawers is the highest mountain in Perthshire. But with a visitor centre and large car park at 430 m, it is one of the most readily accessible sites to see mountain ringlet. This hardy alpine butterfly only flies at altitudes above 350 m. Mountain ringlets can be found on south-facing slopes along the one-mile circular nature trail departing from the visitor centre.

3 ST ABB'S HEAD NATIONAL NATURE RESERVE SOUTH SCOT
Berwickshire *Grid Ref 913674*
www.nnr-scotland.org.uk
St Abb's Head is known as a picturesque clifftop walk and a fantastic seabird

spectacle. However, the reserve is also a superb site for several species of butterfly, most notably northern brown argus. A designated area (with an interpretational panel) is specifically managed for northern brown argus. However, I have always been rewarded with impressive encounters along the south-west-facing slope of the Mire Loch.

4 SEATON CLIFFS WILDLIFE RESERVE PAD&F Angus
Grid Ref NO 667416 www.swt.org.uk
A variety of butterflies have been recorded on the grassy slopes, but for many the real draw is Britain's smallest butterfly, the small blue. These butterflies are easily overlooked as they are more dusky brown than blue and confined to discrete colonies.

5 TAYNISH NATIONAL NATURE RESERVE WHLLS&T Argyllshire
Grid Ref NR 737853
www.nnr-scotland.org.uk
More than 20 species of butterfly have been recorded on the reserve. The most spectacular of these is the marsh fritillary, a large colony of which is found on the coastal grassland at the southern end of the peninsula.

132 OVERNIGHT STAYS FOR BIKERS

1 GOLF LINKS HOTEL HIGHLANDS
Church Street, Golspie 01408 633 408
www.golflinkshotel.co.uk
Ewan McGregor's *Long Way Down* journey started from John o' Groats and headed south. A great place to stop in these parts is the Golf Links hotel in Golspie. Why not road-test a few of

their 150 malt whiskies and savour the sea view too?

2 SCARINISH HOTEL WHLLS&T
Scarinish, Isle of Tiree, Argyll
01879 220 308
www.tireescarinishhotel.com
The family running this place are keen bikers, so they know exactly what to provide for guests. They really will go the extra mile, with great little extras such as sturdy hangers for heavy biking gear and shortbread in the shape of motorbikes.

3 SOLUIS MU THUATH GUESTHOUSE HIGHLANDS
Braeintra, by Achmore, Lochalsh
01599 577 219
www.highlandsaccommodation.co.uk
This little gem nestles in one of Scotland's prettiest spots – a favourite for bikers. To make it even more tempting to visit, the owners offer a drying room, hard-standing parking within gated premises, packed lunches and evening meals with a table licence so you can relax with a nice cold beer.

4 EAST BRAE BED & BREAKFAST
SOUTH SCOT **Crocketford, Dumfries**
01556 690 296
Six miles from Dumfries and 12 from Castle Douglas, East Brae is the perfect stop of for those wanting to spend time exploring the south-west coast. It's already a popular choice for bikers who enjoy the extra facilities such as evening meals, garage parking and drying facilities, but also a warm smile and famously hearty breakfasts.

5 FOUR SEASONS HOTEL PAD&F
St Fillans, Perthshire 01764 685 333
www.thefourseasonshotel.co.uk

The Four Seasons is a favourite for all kinds of visitors enjoying a glorious location on the east side of Loch Earn and motorbikers are no exception. In addition to all the drying and parking facilities, the hotel will also wash biking equipment on request, can provide garage facilities for those that need any repairs and they also provide lots of information about what the local area has to offer.

133 WOODLAND WALKS

1 GATEHOUSE OF FLEET SOUTH SCOT
Kirkcudbrightshire
www.gatehouse-of-fleet.co.uk
A wide range of walks of varying lengths are on offer at Gatehouse of Fleet. A good walk through the beautiful Cally Oak Woods provides a refreshing escape as the colours change and the leaves fall.

2 BALLINDALLOCH CASTLE
ABER/GRAMP **Banffshire**
www.ballindallochcastle.co.uk
Set in the heart of Speyside, Ballindalloch Castle is open to the public and has arguably the biggest Sitka spruce (by girth) in the country. It's also an opportunity to collect conkers. Just don't damage the trees by throwing sticks at the branches.

3 CROOKEDSTANE RIG GLAS/CLYDE
Lanarkshire *www.crookedstane.com*
For those really needing to get away from it all, there is a Meditation Walk at Crookedstane Rig, Lanarkshire. Walkers are welcome in small groups by appointment. A wildlife/botanical guide and map is available to buy. Although it

is rough terrain and quite hilly in places, there are rewarding views over the whole of the southern uplands from the top of Tomont Hill.

4 SCONE PALACE PAD&F
Perthshire *www.scone-palace.net/palace/ grounds.cfm*
The grounds of historic Scone Palace contain a little bit of forestry history. At the end of an avenue of lime trees is a Douglas fir raised from the original seed sent home by David Douglas from America in 1826. David Douglas was born at Scone and worked as an under-gardener here before gaining fame as a plant explorer and collector for the Royal Horticultural Society. The Pinetum provides colour throughout the year and began with the planting of exotic trees in 1848.

5 BLAIR ATHOLL PAD&F
Perthshire
www.athollestatesrangerservice.co.uk
The estate offers many different walks, covering all distances and abilities. An easy woodland walk provides a good chance of seeing red squirrels and a longer walk, all on good tracks, takes you through the woods and out on to the open moor. Pick up a booklet from the Glen Tilt Car Park near Blair Atholl or contact the Atholl Estates Ranger Service for more detailed advice.

134 FISHMONGERS

1 EDDIE'S SEAFOOD MARKET
EDIN/LOTH **7 Roseneath Street, Edinburgh 0131 229 4207**
The queues snaking out on Saturday mornings attest to the popularity of this fishmonger, hailed by Rick Stein in his

book *Seafood Lovers' Guide*. From whiting to monkfish, tuna to lobster (pick your own from the tank), there is every type of fish, exotic and domestic. In fishmonger-style, there is a display in the window, but all eyes stray to the plastic trays which cover most of the floor, each filled with glossy fresh fish, straight from the market. Punters waiting for a salmon steak or scallops stand cheek by jowl with restaurateurs who leave with boxes groaning with treasures. Service is unfussy but friendly. Look out for boxes of sushi on Saturdays, but get there early.

2 CLARK BROS EDIN/LOTH
224 New Street, Musselburgh
0131 665 6181
Often praised by Clarissa Dickson Wright as one of the best fish shops in Scotland, Clark Bros is squeezed in between a petrol station and a health club and function suite, opposite Musselburgh harbour. But inside, it has a delightful array of fish and seafood, beautifully presented, with old favourites and plenty of surprises.

3 KEN WATMOUGH ABER/GRAMP
29 Thistle Street, Aberdeen
01224 640 321
The holder of a Royal Warrant as fishmonger to the Prince of Wales – he also held a Royal Warrant from the Queen Mother – Ken stocks a vast array of fish and shellfish in his small shop near Aberdeen city centre. Celebrity chefs Rick Stein and Delia Smith are fans.

4 KERACHER PAD&F
73 South Street, St Andrews, Fife
01334 472 541 *www.keracher.co.uk*
Poor students in St Andrews (such people do exist) can enjoy a salmon tail

or fillet from Kerachers as a real treat. The shop, with its distinctive round window, always had interesting selections and has an excellent reputation locally.

5 SOMETHING FISHY EDIN/LOTH
16a Broughton Street, Edinburgh
0131 556 7614
Opens 7.30am on weekdays so you can buy fish for dinner and have it marinating before you go to work!

135 GREEN HOLIDAYS

1 PRIVATE YACHT CHARTER
HIGHLANDS **Inner Hebrides**
0131 625 6635
www.wildernessscotland.com
Combine the power of the wind with a bit of legwork and explore the Inner Hebrides. Wilderness Scotland organises yacht charters with skippers and guides to lead you to islands, such as Mull, Iona, Jura and Gigha. You can even travel to Oban by train to minimise your carbon footprint. Wilderness Scotland was the first adventure tour operator in Scotland to gain the gold award in the Green Tourism Business Scheme and recently won the investing in the environment category of the Highlands and Islands Tourism Awards.

2 VISIT THE VERY NORTH OUT. ISLES
Shetland Isles, Herrislea House Hotel
01595 840 208
www.herrisleahouse.co.uk
Almara B&B 01806 503 261
www.almara.shetland.co.uk
You can travel by ferry from Aberdeen, and to Aberdeen by train. Once there, base yourself at Herrislea House Hotel or the Almara B&B. Shetland is a superb place for a walking holiday and also

THE WORD-OF-MOUTH GUIDE TO SCOTLAND

boasts superb wildlife. Visit the Noss National Nature Reserve and Visitor Centre www.nnr-scotland.org to see the bird colonies and don't miss the Jarlshof Historic site www.historic-scotland.gov.uk for a look at Shetland's fascinating history. All of these businesses and attractions have won gold or silver Green Tourism Business Scheme Awards.

3 LEARN TO SEA-KAYAK HIGHLANDS
Torridon 0131 625 6635
www.wildernessscotland.com
Sea-kayaking is a wonderful and low-impact way to experience Scotland's great outdoors. Wilderness Scotland runs trips based at a private bunkhouse in Torridon. The trip starts at Inverness station and a short journey by minibus takes us to Torridon, with a quick stop in Lochcarron to collect the locally-sourced food for the break. As well as enjoying some wonderful sea-kayaking and learning the basic skills, our expert guides will explain 'leave no trace' techniques, helping you reduce your impact while visiting fragile environments.

4 TOUR SCOTLAND WITH RABBIE'S TRAIL BURNERS HIGHLANDS
0131 226 3133 *www.rabbies.com*
Travelling in low emission Mercedes mini-coaches, Rabbie's offers a range of small group tours of the Highlands and Islands, exploring the back roads with their knowledgeable guides. Rabbie's works with accommodation providers to support local communities and holds a gold award in the Green Tourism Business Scheme. By travelling in a small group, rather than in your car, you can reduce your carbon emissions by up to 75 per cent.

5 EXPLORE THE CENTRAL BELT
GLAS/CLYDE **New Lanark Mill**
01555 667 200 *www.newlanark.org and www.newlanarkhotel.co.uk*
Basing yourself in one of the self-catering cottages at the New Lanark Mill, a World Heritage Site, you can step back in time in just a short journey from Edinburgh or Glasgow. Bothwell Castle www.historic-scotland.gov.uk is fairly close by if you want to keep the historical theme going. You can even explore the David Livingstone Centre www.nts.org.uk at Blantyre for a taste of his incredible journeys. For wildlife lovers or to stretch your legs, the Falls of Clyde www.swt.org.uk is now part of a National Nature Reserve and well worth a visit. These attractions can also be visited in a day from home: but make sure you fill your car with friends to reduce emissions, or cycle!

136 GEOLOGICAL WONDERS

1 THE STORR AND THE QUIRAING
HIGHLANDS **north Skye**
While the whole of the Isle of Skye might be considered a geological wonder, one of the outstanding features has to be the Quiraing and the Storr in the north. A labyrinth of shattered rocks has been created by ancient and repeated giant landslides. An almost Alpine path from the high point on the Uig-Staffin road leads you into the dramatic pinnacles and rock structures.

2 VOLCANIC RING SYSTEM
HIGHLANDS **Ardnamurchan**
Ardnamurchan, at the very west of mainland Britain, consists of one enormous volcanic peninsula. When

141

viewed as an aerial photographic or geological map, the circular forms of the volcanic ring dykes are clearly seen. The best way to see the volcanic system is to take the footpath just by the little hamlet of Achnaha on the road to Sanna Bay, head for Glendrian, a deserted township well worth a little explore, and realise all around you is the magma ring dyke system.

3 FINGAL'S CAVE WHLLS&T
Staffa
Another volcanic feature, this sea cave on the uninhabited island of Staffa is famous both for its hexagonal basalt columns (similar to the more famous Giant's Causeway in Northern Ireland) and also from the 'Hebridean Overture' by Mendelssohn from which it got its name. It is owned by the National Trust for Scotland. One of the easiest ways to visit is to take a boat trip from Iona.

4 PARALLEL ROADS HIGHLANDS
Glen Roy
The Parallel Roads are a series of loch shorelines caused by alternate creation and draining of lochs during the Ice Age, being dammed by glaciers and then draining away as the glaciers melted. A drive up the scenic single track road to Glen Roy near Roy Bridge will let you view the Parallel Roads.

5 OLD MAN OF STOER HIGHLANDS
Sutherland
It's a wonderful walk to view this stack but choose a day that's not too windy as the best way to see it is from the cliff edge. Take the single track road past Culkein and Rubha Stoer and follow it to the end then simply follow the coast north towards Stoer lighthouse till the Old Man of Stoer comes into view.

137 NINE-HOLE GOLF COURSES

1 TOBERMORY WHLLS&T
Mull *4,890 yards, Par 64* **01688 302 743**
www.tobermorygolfclub.com
If man and nature ever conspired to create the perfect golf course, it must have been at Tobermory. From various tees, the view captures Tobermory Bay, the Sound of Mull, Morvern, Ardnamurchan and even, on fine days, the mountains of Rum and Eigg. Approach the signature seventh with care. It is a hole with sharp teeth and is always ready to bite. A short par 3, it demands a pinpoint tee shot to a small green on the far side of the gully. Simply divine.

2 DURNESS HIGHLANDS
Sutherland *5,555 yards, Par 70*
01971 511 364
www.durnessgolfclub.org
Durness is the most northerly course on the mainland, looking out over the beach and Atlantic Ocean. Seals, porpoises and otters can all be seen around the course. It offers relaxed but challenging golf in peaceful, picturesque surroundings. The signature hole, number nine, is a short par three played across the Atlantic – not for the faint-hearted!

3 STRATHTAY PAD&F
Pitlochry *3,774 yards, Par 61*
01887 840 211
The Strathtay course is loved by everyone who has been fortunate enough to play it. The views from the sixth and eighth tees alone are worth the green fee. The brilliant signature-hole fifth, Spion Kop, is played up a

steep hill to a hidden green in a hollow over the summit. Established in 1909, Strathtay will test your shot-making and make you use every club in your bag.

4 CUPAR PAD&F
Fife *5,153 yards, Par 68* **01334 653 549**
www.cupargolfclub.co.uk
One must-see destination on any Fife golf tour is Cupar golf course. Founded in 1855, this is believed to be the oldest nine-hole course in the world. Lee Trevino and Eric Thomson are among the many who have made the pilgrimage there. This parkland course sits upon the Hill of Tarvit, offering great views of the village. One of our most challenging nine-hole courses.

5 DUNNING PAD&F
Perthshire *4,777 yards, Par 66*
01764 684 747
One of the most popular courses in Perthshire is Dunning. This short but challenging parkland course has a series of stone-built bridges crossing a burn that comes into play on a number of holes. Being accurate off the tee is paramount to shooting a good score. The tight-driving first hole, the Avenue, is the signature hole, with mature trees on both sides to a slightly sloping and well guarded green.

MY RECOMMENDATIONS

....

....

....

....

....

....

....

....

....

....

....

Please send us your recommendations by emailing
readersrecommend@scotsman.com
or writing to me at *The Scotsman*,
108 Holyrood Road, Edinburgh, EH8 8AS or by logging on to
www.scotsman.com/recommends

Index by Category

À la carte eating 131
Afternoon teas 85
All-day walks 110
Alternative tourist attractions 116
Bed and breakfasts 78
Bike rides 113
Birdwatching sites 33
Birthplaces to visit 71
Boating ponds 55
Bookshops 14
Breakfasts 48
Brochs 30
Butchers 34
Cafés 125
Campsites 81
Cathedrals 106
Caves 13
Cheap golf hotels 124
Cheap places to eat 16
Cheese shops 57
Chinese food 113
Chocolatiers 48
City viewpoints 56
Climbing for beginners 75
Coastal painters 123
Coastal walks 126
Coffee shops 96
Contemporary buildings 89
Country house hotels 96
Country parks 120
Crêpes 44
Days out on Royal Deeside 92
Delicatessens 13
Dive sites 31
Dog-friendly hotels 118
Dog walking 130
Edin-burgers 122

Extreme points of Scotland 82
Fairtrade clothes 92
Family walks 19
Famous trees 88
Farm shops/farmers' markets 36
Ferry journeys 105
Film locations 68
Fish and chips 15
Fishing for beginners 58
Fishing villages 108
Fishmongers 139
Florists 85
Free things to do with children 28
French restaurants 32
Garden centres 132
Gardens 43
Geological wonders 141
Glasshouses 39
Glens 98
Great roads for bikers 61
Great wedding locations 83
Green holidays 140
Hidden shopping gems 52
High-level drives 45
Hotel bars 94
Ice cream 20
Independent wine shops 38
Indian food 87
Intriguing place names 127
Island towns 52
Italian restaurants 24
Japanese food 70
Jazz venues 103
Land-based dolphin watching 132
Lochs 133

Munros for novices 21
Museums 105
Nine-hole golf courses 143
Old-fashioned pubs 46
Outdoor activity operators 109
Overnight stays for bikers 138
Pine forests 80
Pizzas 104
Places for steam enthusiasts 124
Places for teenagers to eat 60
Places to build sandcastles 73
Places to buy Christmas cards 128
Places to feed ducks 129
Places to find conkers 81
Places to fly kites 119
Places to propose 95
Places to see autumn leaves 86
Places to see owls 28
Places to see rare butterflies 137
Places to see red squirrels 115
Places to see salmon leaping 53
Places to see the red deer rut 100
Places to skim stones 18
Playparks 23
Pre-theatre meals 62
Quiet beaches 40
Real cider pubs 26
Roadside food 78

Robert Burns sites 25
Romantic restaurants 50
Rugby grounds 63
Runs 136
Sailing and fine dining 97
Sandwich bars 20
Scots words 99
Sculptures 135
Seabird-watching 110
Seafood restaurants 59
Sealife centres 99
Self-catering cottages 15
Shoe shops 79
Shops to buy Christmas
    decorations 120
Small cinemas 73
Sports shops 91
Spots for stargazing 47
Style bars 42
Sunday lunches 72
Surfing beaches 65
Sweet shops 59
Thai food 136
Toilets 64
Toyshops 63
Traditional music venues 25
Train journeys 49
Vegetarian restaurants 89
Victorian spa towns 57
Walkers' bars 66
War memorials 114
Watercolour artists 93
Waterfalls 129
Waterside walks 76
Wild places 34
Winter youth hostels 27
Wishing wells and trees 67
Woodland walks 139

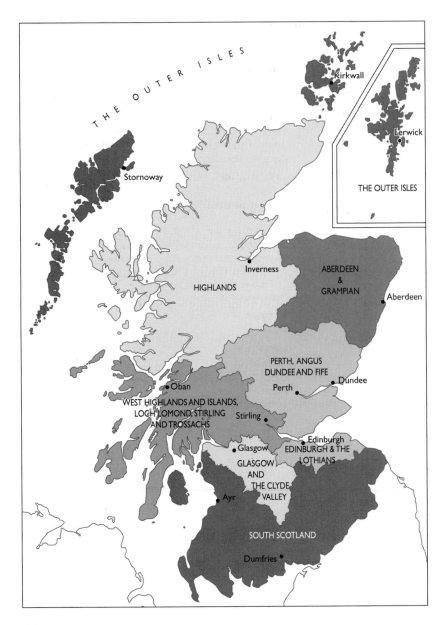

THE OUTER ISLES

Kirkwall

Lerwick

THE OUTER ISLES

Stornoway

Inverness

ABERDEEN
&
GRAMPIAN

HIGHLANDS

Aberdeen

PERTH, ANGUS
DUNDEE AND FIFE

Oban

Dundee

Perth

WEST HIGHLANDS AND ISLANDS,
LOCH LOMOND, STIRLING
AND TROSSACHS

Stirling

Edinburgh

Glasgow

EDINBURGH & THE
LOTHIANS

GLASGOW
AND
THE CLYDE
VALLEY

Ayr

SOUTH SCOTLAND

Dumfries

Index by Area

1 THE OUTER ISLANDS
(Shetland, Orkney and the Outer Hebrides)

ORKNEY
Alternative tourist attractions 116
Birdwatching sites 33
Brochs 30
Cathedrals 106
Ferry journeys 105
Island towns 52
Places to see owls 28
Seabird-watching 110

SHETLAND
Brochs 30
Extreme points of Scotland 82
Green holidays 140
Seabird-watching 110

BARRA
Ferry journeys 105
Quiet beaches 40
War memorials 114

HARRIS
Cafés 125
Self-catering cottages 15

LEWIS
Brochs 30
Butchers 34
Ferry journeys 105
Island towns 52
Places to see owls 28
Quiet beaches 40
Runs 136
Surfing beaches 65
Thai food 136

NORTH UIST
Island towns 52

2 THE HIGHLANDS

ABERNETHY
Birdwatching sites 33
Pine forests 80

ACHILTIBUIE
Cafés 125
Intriguing place names 127
Places to skim stones 18

ARDNAMURCHAN
Caves 13
Extreme points of Scotland 82
Geological wonders 141
Intriguing place names 127
Land-based dolphin watching 132
Quiet beaches 40
Wild places 34

ASSYNT
Lochs 133

AVIEMORE
Cafés 125
Garden centres 132
Places for steam enthusiasts 124
Spots for stargazing 47
Winter youth hostels 27

CAIRNGORMS
Glens 98
Great wedding locations 83
Lochs 133

CULLODEN
Wishing wells and trees 67

DULNAIN BRIDGE
Country house hotels 96

DUNNET HEAD
Extreme points of Scotland 82

DURNESS
Nine-hole golf courses 143

EASTER ROSS
Birthplaces to visit 71
Chocolatiers 48
Intriguing place names 127
Land-based dolphin watching 132
Victorian spa towns 57
Wishing wells and trees 67

FORT WILLIAM
Bed and breakfasts 78
Outdoor activity operators 109
Places for steam enthusiasts 124
Walkers' bars 66

GLEN AFFRIC
Glens 98
Pine forests 80

GLENCOE
Glens 98
Great roads for bikers 61
Walkers' bars 66

GLENMORE FOREST
Pine forests 80
Places to see red squirrels 115

GLEN NEVIS
Climbing for beginners 75
Film locations 68
Waterfalls 129

GOLSPIE
Overnight stays for bikers 138

INCHNADAMPH
Caves 13

INVERNESS
Bike rides 113
Bookshops 14
Butchers 34
Cheap places to eat 16
Cheese shops 57
Chocolatiers 48
City viewpoints 56
Museums 105
Places to fly kites 119
Places to see autumn
  leaves 86
Traditional music venues 25
Train journeys 49

INVERNESS-SHIRE
Places to see rare
  butterflies 137

KINGUSSIE
Places to see the red deer
  rut 100

KINTAIL
Waterfalls 129

LAIRG
Outdoor activity operators
  109

LOCHABER
Brochs 30
Lochs 133
Places to skim stones 18

LOCHALSH
Overnight stays for bikers
  138

MALLAIG
Places for steam
  enthusiasts 124

NAIRN
Places to build sandcastles
  73
Spots for stargazing 47

RANNOCH MOOR
Film locations 68
Great roads for bikers 61

SKYE
Climbing for beginners 75
Ferry journeys 105
Geological wonders 141
Glens 98
Great roads for bikers 61
Island towns 52
Old-fashioned pubs 46
Quiet beaches 40
Self-catering cottages 15
Toilets (Kyle of Lochalsh) 64
Walkers' bars 66
Waterfalls 129
Wild places 34

SPEAN BRIDGE
Geological wonders 141
Sculptures 135

SPEYSIDE
Woodland walks 139

SUTHERLAND
Chocolatiers 48
Contemporary buildings 89
Geological wonders 141
Intriguing place names 127
Places to see salmon
  leaping 53
Surfing beaches 65
Waterfalls 129
Wild places 34

THURSO/WICK
Ferry journeys 105
Jazz venues 103
Surfing beaches 65

TORRIDON
Green holidays 140

WESTERN HIGHLANDS
Campsites 81
Pine forests 80
Train journeys 49

WESTER ROSS
Climbing for beginners 75
Ferry journeys 105
Great roads for bikers 61
High-level drives 45
Self-catering cottages 15
Waterfalls 129
Wishing wells and trees 67

**3 ABERDEEN AND
GRAMPIAN**

ABERDEEN CITY
All-day walks 110
City viewpoints 56
Fishing villages 108
Fishmongers 139
Fish and chips 15
Glasshouses 39
Intriguing place names 127
Italian restaurants 24
Japanese food 70
Land-based dolphin
  watching 132
Museums 105
Old-fashioned pubs 46
Shops to buy Christmas
  decorations 120
Sports shops 91
Waterside walks 76
Winter youth hostels 27

**ABERDEENSHIRE
GENERAL/RURAL**
Days out on Royal Deeside
  92
High-level drives 45
Places to see owls 28

Some other books published by Luath Press

ON THE TRAIL OF

On the Trail of John Muir
Cherry Good
ISBN 0 946487 62 6 PBK £7.99

On the Trail of Queen Victoria in the Highlands
Ian R Mitchell
ISBN 0 946487 79 0 PBK £7.99

On the Trail of Robert Burns
John Cairney
ISBN 0 946487 51 0 PBK £7.99

On The Trail of Robert the Bruce
David R. Ross
ISBN 0 946487 52 9 PBK £7.99

On the Trail of William Wallace
David R. Ross
ISBN 0 946487 47 2 PBK £7.99

THE QUEST FOR

The Quest for the Wicker Man
ed. Benjamin Franks et al
ISBN 1 905222 18 1 HBK £16.99

The Quest for Charles Rennie Mackintosh
John Cairney
ISBN 1 905222 43 2 PBK £8.99

LUATH GUIDES TO SCOTLAND

South West Scotland
Tom Atkinson
ISBN 1 905222 15 7 PBK £6.99

Mull & Iona: Highways and Byways
Peter Macnab
ISBN 1 842820 89 3 PBK £5.99

The West Highlands: The Lonely Lands
Tom Atkinson
ISBN 1 84282 088 5 PBK £6.99

The Northern Highlands: The Empty Lands
Tom Atkinson
ISBN 1 84282 087 7 PBK £6.99

The North West Highlands: Roads to the Isles
Tom Atkinson
ISBN 1 84282 086 9 PBK £6.99

TRAVEL AND LEISURE

The Art of Putting
Willie Park Junior
ISBN 1 905222 66 1 PBK £5.99

The Game of Golf
Willie Park Junior
ISBN 1 905222 65 3 HBK £16.99

Riddoch on the Outer Hebrides
Lesley Riddoch
ISBN 1 905222 99 8 PBK £12.99

Loch Lomond and the Trossachs: A complete A-Z of Loch Lomond & the Trossachs National Park and surrounding area
John Barrington
ISBN 1 905222 42 4 PBK £8.99

FOOD AND DRINK

The Ultimate Burns Supper Book
Clark McGinn
ISBN 1 905222 60 2 PBK £7.99

The Whisky Muse: Scotch whisky in poem & song
Robin Laing
ISBN 1 84282 041 9 PBK £7.99

The Whisky River: Distilleries of Speyside
Robin Laing
ISBN 1 905222 97 1 PBK £12.99

NATURAL WORLD

Wild Lives: A Herd of Red Deer
Frank Fraser Darling
ISBN 1 906307 42 3 PBK £9.99

Wild Scotland: essential guide to the best of natural Scotland
James McCarthy
ISBN 1 84282 096 6 PBK £8.99

Luath Press Limited

committed to publishing well written books worth reading

LUATH PRESS takes its name from Robert Burns, whose little collie Luath (*Gael.*, swift or nimble) tripped up Jean Armour at a wedding and gave him the chance to speak to the woman who was to be his wife and the abiding love of his life. Burns called one of 'The Twa Dogs' Luath after Cuchullin's hunting dog in Ossian's *Fingal*. Luath Press was established in 1981 in the heart of Burns country, and now resides a few steps up the road from Burns' first lodgings on Edinburgh's Royal Mile.

Luath offers you distinctive writing with a hint of unexpected pleasures.

Most bookshops in the UK, the US, Canada, Australia, New Zealand and parts of Europe either carry our books in stock or can order them for you. To order direct from us, please send a £sterling cheque, postal order, international money order or your credit card details (number, address of cardholder and expiry date) to us at the address below. Please add post and packing as follows: UK – £1.00 per delivery address; overseas surface mail – £2.50 per delivery address; overseas airmail – £3.50 for the first book to each delivery address, plus £1.00 for each additional book by airmail to the same address. If your order is a gift, we will happily enclose your card or message at no extra charge.

Luath Press Limited

543/2 Castlehill
The Royal Mile
Edinburgh EH1 2ND
Scotland
Telephone: 0131 225 4326 (24 hours)
Fax: 0131 225 4324
email: sales@luath.co.uk
Website: www.luath.co.uk

Old-fashioned pubs 46
Pizzas 104
Places for teenagers to eat 60
Places to buy Christmas cards 128
Places to find conkers 81
Places to propose 95
Playparks 23
Pre-theatre meals 62
Real cider pubs 26
Roadside food 78
Romantic restaurants 50
Rugby grounds 63
Runs 136
Sandwich bars 20
Sculptures 135
Seafood restaurants 59
Shoe shops 79
Shops to buy Christmas decorations 120
Small cinemas 73
Sports shops 91
Spots for stargazing 47
Style bars 42
Sweet shops 59
Thai food 136
Toilets 64
Toyshops 63
Train journeys 49
Traditional music venues 25
Vegetarian restaurants 89
Winter youth hostels 27
Waterside walks 76
Watercolour artists 93

EAST LOTHIAN GENERAL
All-day walks 110

DUNBAR
Birthplaces to visit 71

Dive sites 31
Family walks 19

EAST FORTUNE
Garden centres 132

EAST LINTON
Garden centres 132

GULLANE
Dog-friendly hotels 118
Sunday lunches 72

LONGNIDDRY
Dog walking 130
Places to build sandcastles 73
Quiet beaches 40
Sandwich bars 20

MUSSELBURGH
Bike rides 113
Fishmongers 139
Ice cream 20
Places to feed ducks 129
Places to find conkers 81
Thai food 136
Toilets 64

NORTH BERWICK
Dive sites 31
Farm shops/farmers' markets 36
Free things to do with children 28
Independent wine shops 38
Italian restaurants 24
Pizzas 104
Sealife centres 99

PEASE BAY
Surfing beaches 65

PORT SETON
Coastal painters 123

TRAPRAIN LAW
Climbing for beginners 75

MIDLOTHIAN

DALKEITH
Places to see autumn leaves 86

FLOTTERSTONE
Family walks 19

LASSWADE
Places to buy Christmas cards 128

LOANHEAD
Garden centres 132

MIDDLETON
High-level drives 45

SOUTRA
High-level drives 45

VOGRIE COUNTRY PARK
Country parks 120
Playparks 23

WEST LOTHIAN

LINLITHGOW
Jazz venues 103
Watercolour artists 93
Waterside walks 76

LIVINGSTON
Chinese food 113

MID-CALDER
Country parks 120

NEWTON
Garden centres 132

PUMPHERSTON
Chinese food 113

SOUTH QUEENSFERRY
Bike rides 113
Farm shops/farmers'
    markets 36
Places to find conkers 81
Romantic restaurants 50

7 GREATER GLASGOW
& CLYDE VALLEY
GLASGOW
À la carte eating 131
Afternoon teas 85
Bike rides 113
Bookshops 14
Breakfasts 48
Cheap places to eat 16
Cheese shops 57
City viewpoints 56
Crêpes 44
Coffee shops 96
Contemporary buildings 89
Delicatessens 13
Fairtrade clothes 92
Film locations 68
Florists 85
French restaurants 32
Glasshouses 39
Hidden shopping gems 52
Hotel bars 94
Indian food 87
Italian restaurants 24
Japanese food 70
Museums 105
Old-fashioned pubs 46
Places to buy Christmas
    cards 128
Places to find conkers 81
Places for steam
    enthusiasts 124
Playparks 23

Pre-theatre meals 62
Real cider pubs 26
Rugby grounds 63
Sculptures 135
Shoe shops 79
Shops to buy Christmas
    decorations 120
Small cinemas 73
Sports shops 91
Style bars 42
Toilets 64
Toyshops 63
Traditional music venues
    25
Train journeys 49
Vegetarian restaurants 89
Winter youth hostels 27

EAST DUNBARTONSHIRE
Country parks 120

LANARKSHIRE GENERAL
High-level drives 45

BOTHWELL
Romantic restaurants 50

CROSSWOODHILL FARM
Self-catering cottages 15

EAST KILBRIDE
Contemporary buildings 89

FALLS OF CLYDE
Places to see owls 28
Waterside walks 76

HAMILTON
Country parks 120
Ice cream 20

NEW LANARK
Green holidays 140

RENFREWSHIRE
LANGBANK
Playparks 23

PAISLEY
Hotel bars 94

8 SOUTH OF SCOTLAND
AYRSHIRE & ARRAN
ARRAN
Caves 13
Cheese shops 57
Family walks 19
Famous trees 88
Outdoor activity operators
    109
Places to see red squirrels
    115
Walkers' bars 66

ALLOWAY
Birthplaces to visit 71
Robert Burns sites 25

AYR
Train journeys 49

DUNURE/CROY BAY
Alternative tourist
    attractions 116

ISLE OF CUMBRAE
Bike rides 113

MAIDENS BAY
Places to build sandcastles
    73

STEVENSON
Places to fly kites 119

TROON
Cheap golf hotels 124
Sailing and fine dining 97

DUMFRIES & GALLOWAY

CAERLAVEROCK
Places to see owls 28

DRUMLANRIG
Places to see red squirrels 115

DUMFRIES
Birthplaces to visit 71
Gardens 43
Old-fashioned pubs 46
Overnight stays for bikers 138
Robert Burns sites 25

GALLOWAY FOREST
Places to see the red deer rut 100

GATEHOUSE OF FLEET
Woodland walks 139

ISLE OF WHITHORN
Film locations 68

KIRKCUDBRIGHT
Alternative tourist attractions 116

MOFFAT
Boating ponds 59
Victorian spa towns 57
Sweet shops 59

MULL OF GALLOWAY
Extreme points of Scotland 82

PORT LOGAN
Gardens 43

PORTPATRICK
Campsites 81

STRANRAER
Train journeys 49
Boating ponds 59

WIGTOWN
Bookshops 14

WOOD OF CREE
Places to see owls 28
Birdwatching sites 33

SCOTTISH BORDERS
GENERAL
All-day walks 110

EYEMOUTH
Dive sites 31

INNERLEITHEN
High-level drives 45
Victorian spa towns 57

JEDBURGH
Rugby grounds 63

KELSO
Cheese shops 57
Dog-friendly hotels 118
Places to see autumn leaves 86
Toyshops 63

MELROSE
Great wedding locations 83
Rugby grounds 63

PEEBLES
Cafés 125
Places to see autumn leaves 86
Watercolour artists 93

RIVER TWEED
Fishing for beginners 58

ST ABBS
All-day walks 110
Coastal painters 123
Places to see rare butterflies 137
Seabird-watching 110
Wild places 34

SELKIRK
Places to see salmon leaping 53

Recommends

Every Wednesday in

THE SCOTSMAN

Have you been in it yet?

The Scotsman was founded in 1817 on three cornerstones - impartiality, firmness and independence. Those three core values still hold firm today as the paper connects with readers in a modern and ever-changing world.

Whether you are here for a day, a week or the rest of your life, The Scotsman is the newspaper to find out what's going on in Scotland.

www.scotsman.com

Places to see red squirrels
  115

BALLATER
Country house hotels 96
Days out on Royal Deeside
  92
Victorian spa towns 57

CROVIE
Fishing villages 108

FINZEAN
War memorials 114

FRASERBURGH
Alternative tourist
  attractions 116
Cheap places to eat 16
Surfing beaches 65

GARDENSTOWN
Fishing villages 108

GLENSHEE
Country house hotels 96
Munros for novices 21
Walkers' bars 66

GLEN TANAR
Places to see salmon
  leaping 53

HUNTLY
Gardens 43

NEWBURGH
Cheap golf hotels 124

PENNAN
Film locations 68

PETERHEAD
Extreme points of Scotland
  82

ROSEHEARTY
Intriguing place names 127

STONEHAVEN
Coastal painters 123
Coastal walks 126
Seabird-watching 110

MORAY
All-day walks 110
Coastal walks 126
Intriguing place names 127
  (Portknockie,
  Maggieknockater)
Land-based dolphin
  watching 132

FORRES
Places to feed ducks 129

SANDEND
Fishing villages 108

**4 PERTHSHIRE, ANGUS,
DUNDEE & FIFE**

PERTH & KINROSS

ABERFELDY
Bookshops 14
Cafés 125
High-level drives 45
Places to see the red deer
  rut 100

ABERNETHY
Farm shops/farmers'
  markets 36

AUCHTERARDER
Sandwich bars 20

BALQUHIDDER
Great wedding locations 83

BEN LAWERS
Munros for novices 21
Places to see rare
  butterflies 137

BLAIR ATHOLL
Campsites 81
Woodland walks 139

BRUAR
Farm shops/farmers'
  markets 36
High-level drives 45

COMRIE
Munros for novices 21

CRIEFF
Sweet shops 59
Watercolour artists 93

DUNBLANE
Cathedrals 106

DUNKELD
À la carte eating 131
Family walks 19
Great wedding locations 83
Outdoor activity operators
  109
Places to see autumn
  leaves 86
Places to skim stones 18
Toilets 64

DUNNING
Nine-hole golf courses 143

FALLS OF BRAAN
Places to see salmon
  leaping 53

FORTINGALL
Famous trees 88

GILMERTON
High-level drives 45

KILCHRENAN
Romantic restaurants 50

KINLOCH RANNOCH
High-level drives 45
Munros for novices 21

KINNAIRD ESTATE
Places to propose 95

KINROSS
Farm shops/farmers'
markets 36

LOCH OF THE LOWES
Places to see red squirrels
115

LOCH RANNOCH
Pine forests 80

LOCH TAY
Fishing for beginners 58

METHVEN
Self-catering cottages 15

PERTH
Alternative tourist
attractions 116
Farm shops/farmers'
markets 36
Train journeys 49

PITLOCHRY
Country house hotels 96
Nine-hole golf courses 143
Places to see salmon
leaping 53
Roadside food 78

SCONE
Woodland walks 139

ST FILLANS
Great roads for bikers 61
Overnight stays for bikers
138

ANGUS

ARBROATH
Jazz venues 103

AUCHMITHIE
Places to skim stones 18

BRECHIN
Coffee shops 96

EDZELL
Coffee shops 96
War memorials 114

GLAMIS
Dog-friendly hotels 118

LUNAN BAY
Places to fly kites 119

MONIKIE
Country parks 120

SEATON CLIFFS
Places to see rare
butterflies 137

DUNDEE
Boating ponds 55
Crêpes 44
Cheese shops 57
City viewpoints 56
Contemporary buildings 89
Free things to do with
children 28
Museums 105
Playparks 23
Roadside food 78
Sports shops 91
Spots for stargazing 47
Train journeys 49

BROUGHTY FERRY
Places to skim stones 18
Playparks 23

Places to feed ducks 129
Dog walking 130

FIFE GENERAL
All-day walks 110
Coastal walks 126

ANSTRUTHER
Seafood restaurants 59

AUCHTERMUCHTY
Intriguing place names 127

CELLARDYKE
Fishing villages 108

CUPAR
Nine-hole golf courses 143
Places to see the red deer
rut 100

DUNFERMLINE
Birthplaces to visit 71
Fishing for beginners 58

ELIE
Places to build sandcastles
73

FALKLAND
Great wedding locations 83

FIRTH OF FORTH
Birdwatching sites 33
Free things to do with
children 28
Seabird-watching 110

GLENROTHES
Independent wine shops 38

KIRKCALDY
Places to find conkers 81

LOCHGELLY
Country parks 120

MARKINCH
Romantic restaurants 50

NORTH QUEENSFERRY
Sealife centres 99

ST ANDREWS
Boating ponds 55
Cathedrals 106
Cheap golf hotels 124
Cheese shops 57
Coffee shops 96
Dog-friendly hotels 118
Fishmongers 139
Free things to do with
    children 28
Great wedding locations 83
Hotel bars 94
Ice cream 20
Indian food 87
Jazz venues 103
Places to build sandcastles
    73
Places to feed ducks 129
Places to fly kites 119
Sealife centres 99
Shops to buy Christmas
    decorations 120
Small cinemas 73
Spots for stargazing 47
War memorials 114

ST MONANS
Seafood restaurants 59

WEMYSS
Caves 13

**5 WEST HIGHLANDS &
ISLANDS, LOCH
LOMOND, STIRLING &
TROSSACHS**

ARGYLL

ARDFERN
Sailing and fine dining 97

ARROCHAR
Roadside food 78

BEN CRUACHAN
Alternative tourist
    attractions 116

BUTE
Glasshouses 39

CALLANDER
Great roads for bikers 61
Sweet shops 59

CRINAN CANAL
Alternative tourist
    attractions 116
Sailing and fine dining 97

DUNOON
Butchers 34

INVERAWE
Fishing for beginners 58

KILBERRY
Romantic restaurants 50

KILCHRENAN
Dog-friendly hotels 118

KILMELFORD
Wishing wells and trees 67

KINTYRE
Coastal painters 123

LOCH FYNE
Bed and breakfasts 78
Dive sites 31
Farm shops/farmers'
    markets 36

LOCHGILPHEAD
Sailing and fine dining 97

MACHRINHANISH
Surfing beaches 65

OBAN
Campsites 81
Coastal walks 126
Famous trees 88
Ferry journeys 105
Gardens 43
Green holidays 140
Outdoor activity operators
    109
Sealife centres 99
Sunday lunches 72
Winter youth hostels 27
Wishing wells and trees 67

STRATHLACHLAN
Romantic restaurants 50

TAYNISH
Places to see rare
    butterflies 137

TAYVALLICH
Sailing and fine dining 97

ISLANDS

GIGHA
Gardens 43
Green holidays 140
Runs 136

IONA
Ferry journeys 105
Green holidays 140

ISLAY
Birdwatching sites 33
Land-based dolphin
    watching 132
Runs 136

MULL
Ferry journeys 105
Green holidays 140
Island towns 52
Nine-hole golf courses 143
War memorials 114

STAFFA
Geological wonders 141

TIREE
Overnight stays for bikers 138
Places to fly kites 119
Surfing beaches 65

LOCH LOMOND & TROSSACHS

ABERFOYLE
Wishing wells and trees 67

ARDEN
Bed and breakfasts 78

ARROCHAR
À la carte eating 131

BALLOCH
À la carte eating 131
Country parks 120
Hotel bars 94
Sealife centres 99
Sunday lunches 72

BEN LOMOND
Munros for novices 21

DUMBARTON/ DUNBARTONSHIRE
Alternative tourist attractions 116
Campsites 81
Climbing for beginners 75

INCHLONGAIG
Famous trees 88

LOCH ACHRAY
Waterside walks 76

LOCH KATRINE
Great wedding locations 83
Places to propose 95

STIRLINGSHIRE, FALKIRK & CLACKS

AIRTH
Alternative tourist attractions 116

BO'NESS
Places for steam enthusiasts 124

BRIDGE OF ALLAN
Delicatessens 13
Fish and chips 15
Ice cream 20
Independent wine shops 38
Victorian spa towns 57

DOLLAR
Family walks 19

FALKIRK
Boating ponds 59
Contemporary buildings 89
Fish and chips 15
Great wedding locations 83

FINTRY
High-level drives 45

KIPPEN
High-level drives 45

STIRLING
Alternative tourist attractions 116
Cheap golf hotels 124
Cheap places to eat 16
Dog walking 130
Farm shops/farmers' markets 36
Fishing for beginners 58
High level drives 45
Ice cream 20
Small cinemas 73
Toyshops 63

6 EDINBURGH & LOTHIANS

EDINBURGH
À la carte eating 131
Afternoon teas 85
All-day walks 110
Bed and breakfasts 78
Bike rides 113
Birthplaces to visit 71
Breakfasts 48
Bookshops 14
Butchers 34
Cathedrals 106
City viewpoints 56
Cheap places to eat 16
Chinese food 113
Chocolatiers 48
Climbing for beginners 75
Contemporary buildings 89
Crêpes 44
Delicatessens 13
Dog walking 130
Edin-burgers 122
Fairtrade clothes 92
Farm shops/farmers' markets 36
Film locations 68
Fish and chips 15
Fishmongers 139
Florists 85
Free things to do with children 28
French restaurants 32
Glasshouses 39
Hidden shopping gems 52
Independent wine shops 38
Indian food 87
Italian restaurants 24
Japanese food 70
Jazz venues 103
Museums 105